JOHN LYLY

JOHN LYLY

BY

JOHN DOVER WILSON,

B.A., Late Scholar of Gonville and Caius College, Cambridge.
Members' Prizeman, 1902. Harness Prizeman, 1904.
Honours in Historical Tripos.

HASKELL HOUSE PUBLISHERS Ltd.
Publishers of Scarce Scholarly Books
NEW YORK, N. Y. 10012
1970

First Published 1905

HASKELL HOUSE PUBLISHERS Lᴛᴅ.
Publishers of Scarce Scholarly Books
280 LAFAYETTE STREET
NEW YORK, N. Y. 10012

820.81
L 98 z w

Library of Congress Catalog Card Number: 68-24926

M W

Standard Book Number 8383-0261-0

Printed in the United States of America

PREFACE.

THE following treatise was awarded the *Harness Prize* at Cambridge in 1904. I have, however, revised it since then, and in some matters considerably enlarged it.

A list of the chief authorities to whom I am indebted will be found at the end of the book, but it is fitting that I should here make particular mention of my obligations to the exhaustive work of Mr Bond[1]. Not only have his labours of research and collation lightened the task for me, and for any future student of Lyly, to an incalculable extent, but the various introductory essays scattered up and down his volumes are full of invaluable suggestions.

This book was unfortunately nearing its completion before I was able to avail myself of Mr Martin Hume's *Spanish Influence on English Literature*. But, though I might have added more had his book been accessible earlier, I was glad to find that his conclusions left the main theory of my chapter on Euphuism untouched.

Much as has been written upon John Lyly, no previous critic has attempted to cover the whole ground,

[1] *The Complete Works of John Lyly.* R. W. Bond, 3 Vols. Clarendon Press.

and to sum up in a brief and convenient form the three main literary problems which centre round his name. My solution of these problems may be faulty in detail, but it will I hope be of service to Elizabethan students to have them presented in a single volume and from a single point of view. Furthermore, when I undertook this study, I found several points which seemed to demand closer attention than they had hitherto received. It appeared to me that the last word had not been said even upon the subject of Euphuism, although that topic has usurped the lion's share of critical treatment. And again, while Lyly's claims as a novelist are acknowledged on all hands, I felt that a clear statement of his exact position in the history of our novel was still needed. Finally, inasmuch as the personality of an author is always more fascinating to me than his writings, I determined to attempt to throw some light, however fitful and uncertain, upon the man Lyly himself. The attempt was not entirely fruitless, for it led to the interesting discovery that the fully-developed euphuism was not the creation of Lyly, or Pettie, or indeed of any one individual, but of a circle of young Oxford men which included Gosson, Watson, Hakluyt, and possibly many others.

I have to thank Mr J. R. Collins and Mr J. N. Frazer, the one for help in revision, and the other for assistance in Spanish. But my chief debt of gratitude is due to Dr Ward, the Master of Peterhouse, who has twice read through this book at different stages of its construction. The readiness with which he has put his great learning

at my disposal, his kindly interest, and frequent en-
couragement have been of the very greatest help in a
task which was undertaken and completed under pressure
of other work.

As the full titles of authorities used are to be found
in the list at the end, I have referred to works in the
footnotes simply by the name of their author, while in
quoting from *Euphues* I have throughout employed
Prof. Arber's reprint. Should errors be discovered in
the text I must plead in excuse that, owing to circumstances, the book had to be passed very quickly through
the press.

JOHN DOVER WILSON.

HOLMLEIGH, SHELFORD, *August*, 1905.

TABLE OF CONTENTS.

INTRODUCTION.

CHAPTER I.

CHAPTER II.

CHAPTER III.

CHAPTER IV.

INTRODUCTION.

SINCE the day when Taine established a scientific basis for the historical study of Art, criticism has tended gradually but naturally to fall into two divisions, as distinct from each other as the functions they respectively perform are distinct. The one, which we may call aesthetic criticism, deals with the artist and his works solely for the purpose of interpretation and appreciation, judging them according to some artistic standard, which, as often as not, derives its only sanction from the prejudices of the critic himself. It is of course obvious that, until all critics are agreed upon some common principles of artistic valuation, aesthetic criticism can lay no claim to scientific precision, but must be classed as a department of Art itself. The other, an application of the Darwinian hypothesis to literature, which owes its existence almost entirely to the great French critic before mentioned, but which has since rejected as unscientific many of the laws he formulated, may be called historical or sociological criticism. It judges a work of art, an artist, or an artistic period, on its dynamic and not its intrinsic merits. Its standard is influence, not power or beauty. It is concerned with the artistic qualities of a given artist only in so far as he exerts influence over his successors by those qualities. It is essentially scientific, for it treats the artist as science treats any other natural phenomenon, that is, as the effect of previous causes and

W.   I

the cause of subsequent effects. Its function is one of classification, and with interpretation or appreciation it has nothing to do.

Before undertaking the study of an artist, the critic should carefully distinguish between these two critical methods. A complete study must of course comprehend both ; and in the case of Shakespeare, shall we say, each should be exhaustive. On the other hand, there are artists whose dynamical value is far greater than their intrinsic value, and *vice versa* ; and in such instances the critic must be guided in his action by the relative importance of these values in any particular example. This is so in the case of John Lyly. In the course of the following treatise we shall have occasion to pass many aesthetic judgments upon his work ; but it will be from the historical side that we shall view him in the main, because his importance for the readers of the twentieth century is almost entirely dynamical. His work is by no means devoid of aesthetic merit. He was, like so many of the Elizabethans, a writer of beautiful lyrics which are well known to this day ; but, though the rest of his work is undoubtedly that of an artist of no mean ability, the beauty it possesses is the beauty of a fossil in which few but students would profess any interest. Moreover, even could we claim more for John Lyly than this, any aesthetic criticism would of necessity become a secondary matter in comparison with his importance in other directions, for to the scientific critic he is or should be one of the most significant figures in English literature. This claim I hope to justify in the following pages ; but it will be well, by way of obtaining a broad general view of our subject, to call attention to a few points upon which our justification must ultimately rest.

In the first place John Lyly, inasmuch as he was one

of the earliest writers who considered prose as an artistic end in itself, and not simply as a medium of expression, may be justly described as a founder, if not *the* founder, of English prose style.

In the second place he was the author of the first novel of manners in the language.

And in the third place, and from the point of view of Elizabethan literature most important of all, he was one of our very earliest dramatists, and without doubt merits the title of Father of English Comedy.

It is almost impossible to over-estimate his historical importance in these three departments, and this not because he was a great genius or possessed of any magnificent artistic gifts, but for the simple reason that he happened to stand upon the threshold of modern English literature and at the very entrance to its splendid Elizabethan ante-room, and therefore all who came after felt something of his influence. These are the three chief points of interest about Lyly, but they do not exhaust the problems he presents. We shall have to notice also that as a pamphleteer he becomes entangled in the famous *Marprelate* controversy, and that he was one of the first, being perhaps even earlier than Marlowe, to perceive the value of blank verse for dramatic purposes. Finally, as we have seen, he was the reputed author of some delightful lyrics.

The man of whom one can say such things, the man who showed such versatility and range of expression, the man who took the world by storm and made euphuism the fashion at court before he was well out of his nonage, who for years provided the great Queen with food for laughter, and who was connected with the first ominous outburst of the Puritan spirit, surely possesses personal attractions apart from any literary considerations. We shall presently see reason to believe that his personality was a brilliant and fascinating one. But such a reconstruction of the artist[1] is only possible after a thorough analysis of his works. It would be as well here, however, by way of obtaining an historical framework for our study, to give a brief account of his life as it is known to us.

"Eloquent and witty" John Lyly first saw light in the year 1553 or 1554[2]. Anthony à Wood, the 17th century author of *Athenae Oxonienses*, tells us that he was, like his contemporary Stephen Gosson, a Kentish man born[3]; and with this clue to help them both Mr Bond and Mr Baker are inclined to accept much of the story of Fidus as autobiographical[4]. If their inference be correct, our author would seem to have been the son of middle-class, but well-to-do, parents. But it is with his residence at Oxford that any authentic account of his life must begin, and even then our information is very meagre. Wood tells us that he "became a student in Magdalen College in the beginning of 1569, aged 16 or thereabouts." "And since," adds Mr Bond, "in 1574 he describes himself as Burleigh's alumnus, and owns obligations to him, it is possible that he owed his university career to Burleigh's assistance[5]." And yet, limited as our knowledge is, it is possible, I think, to form a fairly accurate conception of Lyly's manner of life at Oxford, if we are bold enough to read between the lines of the scraps of contemporary evidence that have come down to us. Lyly himself tells us that he left Oxford for three years not long after his arrival. "Oxford," he says, "seemed to weane me before she brought me forth, and to give me boanes to gnawe,

---

[1] Cf. Hennequin. [2] Bond, I. p. 2; Baker, p. v.
[3] *Ath. Ox.* (ed. Bliss), I. p. 676. [4] *Euphues*, p. 268.
[5] Bond, I. p. 6. But Baker, pp. vii, viii, would seem to disagree with this.

before I could get the teate to suck. Wherein she played
the nice mother in sending me into the countrie to nurse,
where I tyred at a drie breast for three years and was at
last inforced to weane myself." Mr Bond, influenced by
the high moral tone of *Euphues*, which, as we shall see,
was merely a traditional literary prose borrowed from the
moral court treatise, is anxious to vindicate Lyly from
all charges of lawlessness, and refuses to admit that the
foregoing words refer to rustication[1]. Lyly's enforced
absence he holds was due to the plague which broke out
at Oxford at this time. Such an interpretation seems
to me to be sufficiently disposed of by the fact that the
plague in question did not break out until 1571[2], while
Lyly's words must refer to a departure (at the very
latest) in 1570. Everything, in fact, goes to show that
he was out of favour with the University authorities.
In the first place he seems to have paid small attention
to his regular studies. To quote Wood again, he was
"always averse to the crabbed studies of Logic and
Philosophy. For so it was that his genie, being naturally
bent to the pleasant paths of poetry (as if Apollo had
given to him a wreath of his own Bays without snatching
or struggling), did in a manner neglect academical studies,
yet not so much but that he took the Degree in Arts,
that of Master being completed in 1575[3]."

Neglect of the recognised studies, however, was not
the only blot upon Lyly's Oxford life. From the hints
thrown out by his contemporaries, and from some
allusions, doubtless personal, in the *Euphues*, we learn
that, as an undergraduate, he was an irresponsible madcap. "Esteemed in the University a noted wit," he
would very naturally become the centre of a pleasure-

---

[1] Bond, I. p. 11.   [2] Baker, p. xii.
[3] *Athenae Oxonienses* (ed. Bliss), I. p. 676.

seeking circle of friends, despising the persons and ideas of their elders, eager to adopt the latest fashion whether in dress or in thought, and intolerant alike of regulations and of duty. Gabriel Harvey, who nursed a grudge against Lyly, even speaks of "horning, gaming, fooling and knaving," words which convey a distinct sense of something discreditable, whatever may be their exact significance. It is necessary to lay stress upon this period of Lyly's life, because, as I hope to show, his residence at Oxford, and the friends he made there, had a profound influence upon his later development, and in particular determined his literary bent. For our present purpose, however, which is merely to give a brief sketch of his life, it is sufficient to notice that our author's conduct during his residence was not so exemplary as it might have been. It must, therefore, have called forth a sigh of relief from the authorities of Magdalen, when they saw the last of John Lyly, M.A., in 1575. He however, quite naturally, saw matters otherwise. It would seem to him that the College was suffering wrong in losing so excellent a wit, and accordingly he heroically took steps to prevent such a catastrophe, for in 1576 we find him writing to his patron Burleigh, requesting him to procure mandatory letters from the Queen "that so under your auspices I may be quietly admitted a Fellow there." The petition was refused, Burleigh's sense of propriety overcoming his sense of humour, and the petitioner quitted Oxford, leaving his College the legacy of an unpaid bill for battels, and probably already preparing in his brain the revenge, which subsequently took the form of an attack upon his University in *Euphues*, which he published in 1578.

It is interesting to learn that in 1579, according to the common practice of that day, he proceeded to his degree of M.A. at Cambridge, though there is no evidence of any residence there[1]. Indeed we know from other sources that in 1578, or perhaps earlier, Lyly had taken up his position at the Savoy Hospital. It seems probable that he became again indebted to Burleigh's generosity for the rooms he occupied here—unless they were hired for him by Burleigh's son-in-law Edward de Vere, Earl of Oxford. This person, though few of his writings are now extant, is nevertheless an interesting figure in Elizabethan literature. The second part of *Euphues* published in 1580, and the *Hekatompathia* of Thomas Watson, are both dedicated to him, and he seems to have acted as patron to most of Lyly's literary associates when they left Oxford for London. Lyly became his private secretary; and as the Earl was himself a dramatist, though his comedies are now lost, his influence must have confirmed in our author those dramatic aspirations, which were probably acquired at Oxford; and we have every reason for believing that Lyly was still his secretary when he was publishing his two first plays, *Campaspe* and *Sapho*, in 1584. But this point will require a fuller treatment at a later stage of our study.

Somewhere about 1585 Fate settled once and for all the lines on which Lyly's genius was to develop, for at that time he became an assistant master at the St Paul's Choir School. Schools, and especially those for choristers, at this time offered excellent opportunities for dramatic production. Lyly in his new position made good use of his chance, and wrote plays for his young scholars to act, drilling them himself, and perhaps frequently appearing personally on the stage. These chorister-actors were connected in a very special way with royal entertain-

[1] Mr Baker however seems to think that his reference to Cambridge (*Euphues*, p. 436) implies a term of residence there. Baker, p. xxii.

ments ; and therefore they and their instructor would be
constantly brought into touch with the Revels' Office.
As we know from his letters to Elizabeth and to Cecil,
the mastership of the Revels was the post Lyly coveted,
and coveted without success, as far as we can tell, until
the end of his life. But these letters also show us that
he was already connected with this office by his position
in the subordinate office of Tents and Toils. The latter,
originally instituted for the purpose of furnishing the
necessaries of royal hunting and campaigning[1], had apparently become amalgamated under a female sovereign
with the Revels' Office, possibly owing to the fact that its
costumes and weapons provided useful material for entertainments and interludes. Another position which, as
Mr Bond shows, was held at one time by Lyly, was that
of reader of new books to the Bishop of London. This
connexion with the censorship of the day is interesting,
as showing how Lyly was drawn into the whirlpool of
the *Marprelate* controversy. Finally we know that he
was elected a member of Parliament on four separate
occasions[2].

These varied occupations are proof of the energy
and versatility of our author, but not one of them can
be described as lucrative. Nor can his publications have
brought him much profit ; for, though both *Euphues* and
its sequel passed through ten editions before his death,
an author in those days received very little of the proceeds of his work. Moreover the publication of his plays
is rather an indication of financial distress than a sign of
prosperity. The two dramas already mentioned were
printed before Lyly's connexion with the Choir School ;
and, when in 1585 he became " vice-master of Poules

---

[1] Bond, I. p. 38.

[2] I have to thank Dr Ward for pointing out to me the interesting fact
that a large proportion of Elizabeth's M.P.'s were royal officials.

and Foolmaster of the Theater," he would be careful to keep his plays out of the publisher's hands, in order to preserve the acting monopoly. It is probable that the tenure of this Actor-manager-schoolmastership marks the height of Lyly's prosperity, and the inhibition of the boys' acting rights in 1591 must have meant a severe financial loss to him. Thus it is only after this date that he is forced to make what he can by the publication of his other plays. The fear of poverty was the more urgent, because he had a wife and family on his hands. And though Mr Bond believes that he found an occupation after 1591 in writing royal entertainments, and though the inhibition on the choristers' acting was removed as early as 1599, yet the last years of Lyly's life were probably full of disappointment. This indeed is confirmed by the bitter tone of his letter to Elizabeth in 1598 in reference to the mastership of the Revels' Office, which he had at last despaired of. The letter in question is sad reading. Beginning with a euphuism and ending in a jest, it tells of a man who still retains, despite all adversity, a courtly mask and a merry tongue, but beneath this brave surface there is visible a despair— almost amounting to anguish—which the forced merriment only renders more pitiable. And the gloom which surrounded his last years was not only due to the distress of poverty. Before his death in 1606 he had seen his novel eclipsed by the new Arcadian fashion, and had watched the rise of a host of rival dramatists, thrusting him aside while they took advantage of his methods. Greatest of them all, as he must have realised, was Shakespeare, the sun of our drama before whom the silver light of his little moon, which had first illumined our darkness, waned and faded away and was to be for centuries forgotten.

CHAPTER I.

EUPHUISM.

It was as a novelist that Lyly first came before the world of English letters. In 1578 he published a volume, bearing the inscription, *Euphues: the anatomy of wyt*, to which was subjoined the attractive advertisement, *very pleasant for all gentlemen to reade, and most necessary to remember.* This book, which was to work a revolution in our literature, was completed in 1580 by a sequel, entitled *Euphues and his England. Euphues*, to combine the two parts under one name, the fruit of Lyly's nonage, seems to have determined the form of his reputation for the Elizabethans; and even to-day it attracts more attention than any other of his works. This probably implies a false estimate of Lyly's comparative merits as a novelist and as a dramatist. But it is not surprising that critics, living in the century of the novel, and with their eyes towards the country pre-eminent in its production, should think and write of Lyly chiefly as the first of English novelists. The bias of the age is as natural and as dangerous an element in criticism as the bias of the individual. But it is not with the modern appraisement of *Euphues* that we are here concerned. Nor need we proceed immediately to a consideration of its position in the history of the English novel.

We have first to deal with its Elizabethan reputation. Had *Euphues* been a still-born child of Lyly's genius, had it produced no effect upon the literature of the age, it would possess nothing but a purely archaeological interest for us to-day. It would still be the first of English novels: but this claim would lose half its significance, did it not carry with it the implication that the book was also the origin of English novel writing. The importance, therefore, of *Euphues* is not so much that it was primary, as that it was primordial; and, to be such, it must have laid its spell in some way or other upon succeeding writers. Our first task is therefore to enquire what this spell was, and to discover whether the attraction of *Euphues* must be ascribed to Lyly's own invention or to artifices which he borrows from others.

While, as I have said, Lyly's name is associated with the novel by most modern critics, it has earned a more widespread reputation among the laity for affectation and mannerisms of style. Indeed, until fifty years ago, Lyly spelt nothing but euphuism, and euphuism meant simply nonsense, clothed in bombast. It was a blind acceptance of these loose ideas which led Sir Walter Scott to create (as a caricature of Lyly) his Sir Piercie Shafton in *The Monastery*—an historical *faux pas* for which he has been since sufficiently called to account. Nevertheless Lyly's reputation had a certain basis of fact, and we may trace the tradition back to Elizabethan days. It is perhaps worth pointing out that, had we no other evidence upon the subject, the survival of this tradition would lead us to suppose that it was Lyly's style more than anything else which appealed to the men of his day. A contemporary confirmation of this may be found in the words of William Webbe. Writing in 1586 of the "great good grace and sweet vogue which

Eloquence hath attained in our Speeche," he declares
that the English language has thus progressed, "because
it hath had the helpe of such rare and singular wits, as
from time to time myght still adde some amendment to
the same.   Among whom I think there is none that will
gainsay, but Master John Lyly hath deservedly moste
high commendations, as he hath stept one steppe further
therein than any either before or since he first began the
wyttie discourse of his *Euphues*, whose works, surely in
respect of his singular eloquence and brave composition
of apt words and sentences, let the learned examine and
make tryall thereof, through all the parts of Rethoricke,
in fitte phrases, in pithy sentences, in galant tropes, in
flowing speeche, in plaine sense, and surely in my
judgment, I think he wyll yeelde him that verdict which
Quintillian giveth of both the best orators Demosthenes
and Tully, that from the one, nothing may be taken
away, to the other nothing may be added[1]."   After such
eulogy, the description of Lyly by another writer as
"alter Tullius anglorum" will not seem strange.   These
praises were not the extravagances of a few uncritical
admirers; they echo the verdict of the age.   Lyly's
enthronement was of short duration—a matter of some
ten years—but, while it lasted, he reigned supreme.
Such literary idolatries are by no means uncommon,
and often hold their ground for a considerable period.
Beside the vogue of Waller, for example, the duration
of Lyly's reputation was comparatively brief.   More
than a century after the publication of his poems,
Waller was hailed by the Sidney Lee of the day in the
Biographia Britannica of 1766, as "the most celebrated
Lyric Poet that England ever produced."   Whence
comes this striking contrast between past glory and

[1] *A discourse of English Poetrie*, Arber's reprint.

present neglect? How is it that a writer once known as the greatest master of English prose, and a poet once named the most conspicuous of English lyrists, are now but names? They have not faded from memory owing to a mere caprice of fashion. Great artists are subject to an ebb and flow of popularity, for which as yet no tidal theory has been offered as an explanation; but like the sea they are ever permanent. The case of our two writers is different. The wheel of time will never bring *Euphues* and *Sacharissa* "to their own again." They are as dead as the Jacobite cause. And for that very reason they are all the more interesting for the literary historian. All writers are conditioned by their environment, but some concern themselves with the essentials, others with the accidents, of that internally constant, but externally unstable, phenomenon, known as humanity. Waller and Lyly were of the latter class. Like jewels suitable to one costume only, they remained in favour just as long as the fashion that created them lasted. Waller was probably inferior to Lyly as an artist, but he happened to strike a vein which was not exhausted until the end of the 18th century; while the vogue of *Euphues*, though at first far-reaching, was soon crossed by new artificialities such as arcadianism. The secret of Waller's influence was that he stereotyped a new poetic form, a form which, in its restraint and precision, was exactly suited to the intellect of the *ancien régime* with its craving for form and its contempt for ideas. The mainspring of Lyly's popularity was that he did in prose what Waller did in poetry.

SECTION I. *The Anatomy of Euphuism.*

The books which have been written upon the characteristics of Lyly's prose are numberless, and far outweigh

the attention given to his power as a novelist, to say
nothing of his dramas[1]. Indeed the absorption of the
critics in the analysis of euphuism seems to have been,
up to a few years ago, definitely injurious to a true
appreciation of our author's position, by blocking the
path to a recognition of his importance in other directions. And yet, in spite of all this, it cannot be said
that any adequate examination of the structure of Lyly's
style appeared until Mr Child took the matter in hand
in 1894[2]. And Mr Child has performed his task so
scientifically and so exhaustively that he has killed the
topic by making any further treatment of it superfluous.
This being the case, a description of the euphuistic style
need not detain us for long. I shall content myself with
the briefest summary of its characteristics, drawing upon
Mr Child for my matter, and referring those who are
desirous of further details to Mr Child's work itself.
We shall then be in a position to proceed to the more
interesting, and as yet unsettled problem, of the origins
of euphuism. The great value of Mr Child's work lies
in the fact that he has at once simplified and amplified
the conclusions of previous investigators. Dr Weymouth[3]
was the first to discover that, beneath the "curtizan-like
painted affectation" of euphuism, there lay a definite
theory of style and a consistent method of procedure.
Dr Landmann carried the analysis still further in his
now famous paper published in the *New Shakespeare
Society's Transactions* (1880–82). But these two, and
those who have followed them, have erred, on the one
hand in implying that euphuism was much more complex

[1] Child, pp. 6–20, for an account of chief writers who have dealt with
euphuism.

[2] *John Lyly and Euphuism.* C. G. Child.

[3] *On Euphuism*, Phil. Soc. Trans., 1870–2.

than it is in reality, and on the other by confining their
attention to single sentences, and so failing to perceive
that the euphuistic method was applicable to the para-
graph, as a whole, no less than to the sentence. And it
is upon these two points that Mr Child's essay is so
specially illuminating. We shall obtain a correct notion
of the "essential character" of the "euphuistic rhetoric,"
he writes, "if we observe that it employs but one simple
principle in practice, and that it applies this, not only to
the ordering of the single sentence, but in every structural
relation[1]": and this simple principle is "the inducement
of artificial emphasis through Antithesis and Repetition—
Antithesis to give pointed expression to the thought,
Repetition to enforce it[2]." When Lyly set out to write
his novel, it seemed that his intention was to produce
a most elaborate essay in antithesis. The book as a
whole, "very pleasant for all gentlemen to read and
most necessary to remember," was itself an antithesis;
the discourses it contains were framed upon the same
plan; the sentences are grouped antithetically; while
the antithesis is pointed by an equally elaborate repetition of ideas, of vowel sounds and of consonant sounds.
Letters, syllables, words, sentences, sentence groups,
paragraphs, all are employed for the purpose of producing the antithetical style now known as euphuism.
An example will serve to make the matter clearer.
Philautus, upbraiding his treacherous friend Euphues
for robbing him of his lady's love, delivers himself of
the following speech: "Although hitherto Euphues
I have shrined thee in my heart for a trusty friend,
I will shunne thee hereafter as a trothless foe, and
although I cannot see in thee less wit than I was wont,
yet do I find less honesty. I perceive at the last

[1] Child, p. 43.   [2] *id.*, p. 44.

(although being deceived it be too late) that musk though it be sweet in the smell is sour in the smack, that the leaf of the cedar tree though it be fair to be seen, yet the syrup depriveth sight—that friendship though it be plighted by the shaking of the hand, yet it is shaken by the fraud of the heart. But thou hast not much to boast of, for as thou hast won a fickle lady, so hast thou lost a faithful friend[1]." It is impossible to give an adequate idea of the euphuistic style save in a lengthy quotation, such as the discourse of Eubulus selected by Mr Child for that purpose[2]; but, within the narrow limits of the passage I have chosen, the main characteristics of euphuism are sufficiently obvious. It should be noticed how one part of a sentence is balanced by another part, and how this balance or "parallelism" is made more pointed by means of alliteration, e.g. "shrined thee for a trusty friend," "shun thee as a trothless foe"; musk "sweet in the smell," "sour in the smack," and so on. The former of these antitheses is an example of transverse alliteration, of which so much is made by Dr Landmann, but which, as Mr Child shows, plays a subordinate, and an entirely mechanical, part in Lyly's style[3]. Lyly's most natural and most usual method of emphasizing is by means of simple alliteration. On the other hand it must be noticed that he employs alliteration for the sake of euphony alone much more frequently than he uses it for the purpose of emphasis. So that we may conclude by saying that simple alliteration forms the basis of the euphuistic diction, just as we have seen antithesis forms the basis of the euphuistic construction. This brief survey of the framework of euphuism is far from being an exhaustive analysis. All that is here attempted is an enumeration

---

[1] *Euphues*, p. 90.　　　[2] Child, p. 39.　　　[3] *id.*, p. 46.

of the most obvious marks of euphuism, as a necessary step to an investigation of its origin, and to a determination of its place in the history of our literature.

Before, however, leaving the subject entirely, we must mention two more characteristics of Lyly's prose which are very noticeable, but which come under the head of ornamental, rather than constructional, devices. The first of these is a peculiar use of the rhetorical interrogation. Lyly makes use of it when he wishes to portray his characters in distress or excitement, and it most frequently occurs in soliloquies. Sometimes we find a string of these interrogations, at others they are answered by sentences beginning " ay but," and occasionally we have the " ay but " sentence with the preceding interrogation missing. I make a special mention of this point, as we shall find it has a certain connexion with the subject of the origins of euphuism.

The other ornamental device is one which has attracted a considerable quantity of attention from critics, and has frequently been taken by itself as the distinguishing mark of euphuism. In point of fact, however, the euphuists shared it with many other writers of their age, though it is doubtful whether anyone carried it to such extravagant lengths as Lyly. It took the form of illustrations and analogies, so excessive and overwhelming that it is difficult to see how even the idlest lady of Elizabeth's court found time or patience to wade through them. They consist first of anecdotes and allusions relating to historical or mythological persons of the ancient world ; some being drawn from Plutarch, Pliny, Ovid, Virgil, and other sources, but many springing simply from Lyly's exuberant fancy. In the second place *Euphues* is a collection of similes borrowed from "a fantastical natural history, a sort of mythology of plants and stones,

to which the most extraordinary virtues are attributed[1]."
" I have heard," says Camilla, bashfully excusing herself
for taking up the cudgels of argument with the learned
Surius, "that the Tortoise in India when the sunne
shineth, swimmeth above the water wyth hyr back, and
being delighted with the fine weather, forgetteth her
selfe until the heate of the sunne so harden her shell,
that she cannot sink when she woulde, whereby she is
caught. And so it may fare with me that in this good
companye displaying my minde, having more regard to
my delight in talking, than to the ears of the hearers, I
forget what I speake, and so be taken in something
I would not utter, which happilye the itchyng ears of
young gentlemen would so canvas that when I would
call it in, I cannot, and so be caught with the Tortoise,
when I would not[2]." And, when she had finished her
discourse, Surius again employs the simile for the purpose
of turning a neat compliment, saying, "Lady, if the Tortoise you spoke of in India were as cunning in swimming,
as you are in speaking, she would neither fear the heate
of the sunne nor the ginne of the Fisher." This is but a
mild example of the "unnatural natural philosophy"
which *Euphues* has made famous. An unending pro-
cession of such similes, often of the most extravagant
nature, runs throughout the book, and sometimes the
development of the plot is made dependent on them.
Thus Lucilla hesitates to forsake Philautus for Euphues,
because she feels that her new lover will remember "that
the glasse once chased will with the least clappe be
cracked, that the cloth which stayneth with milke will
soon loose his coulour with Vinegar; that the eagle's
wing will waste the feather as well as of the Phoenix, as
of the Pheasant: and that she that hath become faith-

---

[1] Jusserand, p. 107.   [2] *Euphues*, p. 402.

lesse to one, will never be faithfull to any[1]." What proof could be more exact, what better example could be given of the methods of concomitant variations? It is precisely the same logical process which induces the savage to wreak his vengeance by melting a waxen image of his enemy, and the farmer to predict a change of weather at the new moon.

Lyly, however, was not concerned with making philosophical generalizations, or scientific laws, about the world in general. His natural, or unnatural, phenomena were simply saturated with moral significance: not that he saw any connexion between the ethical process and the cosmic process, but, like every one of his contemporaries, he employed the facts of animal and vegetable life to point a moral or to help out a sermon. The arguments he used appear to us puerile in their old-world dress, and yet similar ones are to be heard to-day in every pulpit where a smattering of science is used to eke out a poverty of theology. And, to be fair, such reasoning is not confined to pulpits. Even so eminent a writer as Mr Edward Carpenter has been known to moralise on the habits of the wild mustard, irresistibly reminding us of the "Camomill which the more it is trodden and pressed down the more it speedeth[2]." Moreover the *soi-disant* founder of the inductive method, the great Bacon himself, is, as Liebig[3] shows in his amusing and interesting study of the renowned "scientist's" scientific methods, tarred with the same mediaeval brush, and should be ranked with Lyly and the other Elizabethan "scholastics" rather than with men like Harvey and Newton.

[1] *Euphues*, p. 58.   [2] *id.*, p. 46.
[3] *Lord Bacon et les sciences d'observation en moyen âge*, par Liebig, traduit par de Tchihatchef.

Lyly's natural history was at any rate the result of learning; many of his "facts" were drawn from Pliny, while others were to be found in the plentiful crop of mediaeval bestiaries, which, as Professor Raleigh remarks, "preceded the biological hand-books." Perhaps also we must again allow something for Lyly's invention; for lists of authorities, and footnotes indicative of sources, were not demanded of the scientist of those days, and one can thoroughly sympathise with an author who found an added zest in inventing the facts upon which his theories rested. Have not ethical philosophers of all ages been guilty of it? Certainly Gabriel Harvey seems to be hinting at Lyly when he slyly remarks: "I could name a party, that in comparison of his own inventions, termed Pliny a barren wombe[1]."

The affectations we have just enumerated are much less conspicuous in the second part of *Euphues* than in the first, and, though they find a place in his earlier plays, Lyly gradually frees himself from their influence, owing perhaps to the decline of the euphuistic fashion, but more probably to the growth of his dramatic instinct, which saw that such forms were a drag upon the action of a play. And yet at times Lyly could use his clumsy weapon with great precision and effect. How admirably, for example, does he express in his antithetical fashion the essence of coquetry. Iffida, speaking to Fidus of one she loved but wished to test, is made to say, "I seem straight-laced as one neither accustomed to such suites, nor willing to entertain such a servant, yet so warily, as putting him from me with my little finger, I drewe him to me with my whole hand[2]." Other little delicate turns of phrase may be found in the mine of *Euphues*—for the digging. Our author was no genius, but he had a full

---

[1] Bond, I. p. 131 note.   [2] *Euphues*, p. 299.

measure of that indefinable quality known as wit ; and, though the stylist's mask he wears is uncouth and rigid, it cannot always conceal the twinkle of his eyes Moreover a certain weariness of this sermonizing on the stilts of antithesis is often visible ; and we may suspect that he half sympathises with the petulant exclamation of the sea-sick Philautus to his interminable friend :

"In fayth, Euphues, thou hast told a long tale, the beginning I have forgotten, ye middle I understand not, and the end hangeth not well together[1]"; and with this piece of self-criticism we may leave Lyly for the present and turn to his predecessors.

SECTION II. *The Origins of Euphuism.*

When we pass from an analytical to an historical consideration of the style which Lyly made his own and stamped for ever with the name of his hero, we come upon a problem which is at once the most difficult and the most fascinating with which we have to deal. The search for a solution will lead us far afield ; but, inasmuch as the publication and success of *Euphues* have given euphuism its importance in the history of our literature, the digression, which an attempt to trace the origin of euphuism will necessitate, can hardly be considered outside the scope of this book. Critics have long since decided that the peculiar style, which we have just dissolved into its elements, was not the invention of Lyly's genius ; but on the other hand, no critic, in my opinion, has as yet solved the problem of origins with any claim to finality. Perhaps a tentative solution is all that is possible in the present stage of our knowledge. It is, of course, easy to point to the book or books from

---

[1] *Euphues*, p. 248.

which Lyly borrowed, and to dismiss the question thus.
But this simply evades the whole issue ; for, though it
explains *Euphues*, it by no means explains euphuism.
Equally unsatisfactory is the theory that euphuism was
of purely Spanish origin.   Such a solution has all the
fascination, and all the dangers, which usually attend a
simple answer to a complex question.   The idea that
euphuism was originally an article of foreign production
was first set on foot by Dr Landmann.   The real father
of Lyly's style, he tells us, was Antonio de Guevara,
bishop of Guadix, who published in 1529 a book, the
title of which was as follows : *The book of the emperor
Marcus Aurelius with a Diall for princes*.   This book
was translated into English in 1534 by Lord Berners,
and again in 1557 by Sir Thomas North ; in both cases
from a French version.   The two translations are con-
veniently distinguished by their titles, that of Berners
being *The Golden Boke*, that of North being *The Diall of
Princes*.   Dr Landmann is very positive with regard to
his theory, but the fact that both translations come from
the French and not from the Castilian, seems to me to
constitute a serious drawback to its acceptance.   And
moreover this theory does not explain the really important crux of the whole matter, namely the reason
why a style of this kind, whatever its origin, found a
ready acceptance in England : for fourteen editions of
The Golden Boke are known between 1534 and 1588, a
number for those days quite exceptional and showing
the existence of an eager public.   Two answers are
possible to the last question ; that there existed a large
body of men in the England of the Tudors who were
interested in Spanish literature of all kinds and in
Guevara among others ; and that the euphuistic style
was already forming in England, and that this was the

reason of Guevara's popularity. In both answers I think
there is truth ; and I hope to show that they give us,
when combined, a fairly adequate explanation of the
vogue of euphuism in our country. Let us deal with
external influences first.

The upholders of the Spanish theory have contente
themselves with stating that Lyly borrowed from
Guevara, and pointing out the parallels between the two
writers. But it is possible to give their case a greater
plausibility, by showing that Guevara was no isolated
instance of such Spanish influence, and by proving that
during the Tudor period there was a consistent and
far-reaching interest in Spanish literature among a
certain class of Englishmen. Intimacy with Spain dates
from Henry VIII.'s marriage with Katherine of Aragon,
though no Spanish book had actually been translated
into English before her divorce. But the period from
then onwards until the accession of James I., a period
when Spain looms as largely in English politics as does
France later, saw the publication in London of "some
hundred and seventy volumes written either by peninsular
authors, or in the peninsular tongues[1]." At such a time
this number represents a very considerable influence;
and it is, therefore, no wonder that critics have fallen
victims to the allurements of a theory which would
ascribe Spanish origins for all the various prose epidemics
of Elizabethan literature. To pair Lyly with Guevara,
Sidney with Montemayor[2], and Nash with Mendoza, and
thus to point at Spain as the parent, not only of the
euphuistic, but also of the pastoral and picaresque romance,
is to furnish an explanation almost irresistible in its
symmetry. It must have been with the joy of a

[1] Underhill, p. 339.

[2] id., p. 268 note. Mr Underhill writes: " The attempt to connect the
style of Sidney with that of Montemayor has failed."

mathematician, solving an intricate problem, that Dr Landmann formulated this theory of literary equations. But without going to such lengths, without pressing the connexion between particular writers, one may admit that in general Spanish literature must have exercised an influence upon the Elizabethans. Mr Underhill, our latest authority on the subject, allows this, while at the same time cautioning us against the dangers of over-estimating it. Any contact on the side of the lyric and the drama was, he declares, very slight[1], and the peninsular writings actually circulated in our country at this time, in translations, he divides into three classes; occasional literature, that is topical tracts and pamphlets on contemporary Spanish affairs; didactic literature, comprising scientific treatises, accounts of voyages such as inspired Hakluyt, works on military science, and, more important still, the religious writings of mystics like Granada; and lastly artistic prose. The last item, which alone concerns us, is by far the smallest of the three, and by itself amounts to less than half the translations from Italian literature; moreover most of the Spanish translations under this head came into England after 1580, and could not therefore have influenced Lyly's novel. But of course the *Libro Aureo* had been englished long before this, while the *Lazarillo de Tórmes*, Mendoza's[2] picaresque romance, was given an English garb by Rowland in 1576, and, though Montemayor's *Diana* was not translated until 1596, Spanish and French editions of it had existed in England long previous to that date. Perhaps most important of all was the famous realistic novel *Celestina*, which was well known, in a French translation, to Englishmen at

---

[1] Underhill, p. 48, but see Martin Hume, ch. IX.

[2] Some doubt has been thrown upon Mendoza's authorship. See Fitzmaurice-Kelly, p. 158, and Martin Hume, p. 133.

the beginning of the 16th century, and was denounced by Vives at Oxford. It was actually translated into English as early as 1530[1]. There was on the whole, therefore, quite an appreciable quantity of Spanish artistic literature circulating in England before *Euphues* saw the light.

This literary invasion will seem perfectly natural if we bear in mind the political conditions of the day. Under Mary, England had been all but a Spanish dependency, and, though in the next reign, she threw off the yoke, the antagonism which existed probably acted as an even greater literary stimulus than the former alliance. Throughout the whole of Elizabeth's rule, the English were continually coming into contact with the Spaniards, either in trade, in ecclesiastical matters, in politics, or in actual warfare; and again the magnificence of the great Spanish empire, and the glamour which surrounded its connexion with the new world, were very attractive to the Englishmen of Elizabeth's day, especially as they were desirous of emulating the achievements of Spain. And lastly it may be noticed that English and Spanish conditions of intellectual life, if we shut our eyes to the religious differences, were very similar at this time. Both countries had replaced a shattered feudal system by an absolute and united monarchy. Both countries owed an immense debt to Italy, and, in both, the Italian influence took a similar form, modified on the one hand by humanism, and on the other by feelings of patriotism, if not of imperialism. Spain and England took the Renaissance fever more coldly, and at the same time more seriously, than did Italy. And in both the new movement eventually assumed the character of intellectual asceticism

[1] Martin Hume, p. 126.

moulded by the sombre hand of religious fanaticism; for Spain was the cradle of the Counter-Reformation, England of Puritanism.

Leaving the general issue, let us now try to establish a partial connexion between our author, or at least his surroundings, and Spanish influences. And here I think a suggestive, if not a strong case, can be made out. Ever since the beginning of the 16th century a Spanish tradition had existed at Oxford. Vives, the Spanish humanist, and the friend of Erasmus, was in 1517 admitted Fellow of Corpus Christi College, and in 1523 became reader in rhetoric ; and, though he was banished in 1528, at the time of the divorce, it seems that he was continually lecturing before the University during the five years of his residence there. The circle of his friends, though quite distinct from the contemporary Berners-Guevara group, included many interesting men, and among others the famous Sir John Cheke. Under Mary we naturally find two Spanish professors at Oxford, Pedro de Soto and Juan de Villa Garcia. But Elizabeth maintained the tradition ; and in 1559 she offered a chair at Oxford to a Spanish Protestant, Guerrero. The important name, however, in our connexion is Antonio de Corro, who resided as a student at Christ Church from 1575 to 1585, thus being a contemporary of Lyly, though it is impossible to say whether they were acquainted or not. Lyly had, however, another Oxford contemporary who certainly took a keen interest in Spanish literature, possessing a knowledge of Castilian, though himself an Englishman. This was Hakluyt, who must have been known to Lyly ; and for the following reason. In 1597 Henry Lok[1] published a volume of religious poems to which Lyly contributed commenda-

[1] Bond, I. p. 67.

tory verses. On the other hand Hakluyt's first book
was supplemented by a woodcut map executed by his
friend Michael Lok[1], brother of Thomas Lok the Spanish
merchant, and uncle to the aforesaid Henry. It seems
highly improbable, therefore, that Lyly and Hakluyt
possessing these common friends could have remained
unknown to each other at Oxford. Indeed we may feel
justified in supposing that Hakluyt, Sidney, Carew, Lyly,
Thomas Lodge, and Thomas Rogers (the translator of
Estella) were all personally acquainted, if not intimate,
at the University. Another and very important name
may be added to this list, that of Stephen Gosson, who,
"a Kentish man born" like our hero, and entering
Oxford a year after him (in 1572), must, I feel sure,
have been one of his friends. The fact that he was
at first interested in acting, and is said to have written
comedies, goes a long way to confirm this. We are also
led to suppose that he had devoted some attention to
Spanish literature, and that he was probably acquainted
with Hakluyt and the Loks, from certain verses of his,
printed at the end of Thomas Nicholas' *Pleasant History
of the Conquest of West India*, a translation of Cortes'
book published in 1578[2]. Taking all this into consideration, it is extremely interesting to find Gosson publishing in 1579 his famous *Schoole of Abuse*, which bears
most of the distinguishing marks of euphuism already
noted, but which can scarcely have been modelled upon
Lyly's work ; for as Professor Saintsbury writes : "the
very short interval between the appearance of *Euphues*
and the *Schoole of Abuse*, shows that he must rather
have mastered the Lylian style in the same circumstances

---

[1] Underhill, p. 178, to whom I am indebted for nearly all the preceding
remarks in connexion with the Spanish atmosphere at Oxford.

[2] Arber's reprint, *School of Abuse*, p. 97.

and situations as Lyly than have directly borrowed it from his fellow at Oxford[1]." And moreover Gosson's style does not read like an imitation of Lyly. The same tricks and affectations are employed, but they are employed differently and perhaps more effectively.

Lyly is again found in contact with the Spanish atmosphere, as one of the dependents of the Earl of Oxford, who patronized Robert Baker, George Baker, and Anthony Munday, who were all under the "spell of the peninsula[2]." But we cannot be certain when his relations with de Vere commenced, and unless we can feel sure that they had begun before the writing of *Euphues*, the point is not of importance for our present argument.

These facts are of course little more than hints, but I think they are sufficient to establish a fairly strong probability that Lyly was one of a literary set at Oxford (as I have already suggested in dealing with his life) the members of which were especially interested in Spanish literature, perhaps through the influence of Corro. It seems extremely improbable that Lyly himself possessed any knowledge of Castilian, and it is by no means necessary to show that he did, for it is quite sufficient to point out that he must have been continually in the presence of those who were discussing peninsular writings, and that in this way he would have come to a knowledge of the most famous Spanish book which had yet received translation, the *Libro Aureo* of Guevara.

But we are still left with the question on our hands; why was this book the most famous peninsular production of Lyly's day? It is a question which no critic, as far as I am aware, has ever formulated, and yet it seems endowed with the greatest importance. We have seen how and why Spanish literature in general found

[1] Craik, vol. I. [2] Underhill, ch. VIII. § 2.

a reception in England. But the special question as to the ascendancy of Guevara obviously requires a special answer. Guevara was of course well known all over the continent, and it might seem that this was a sufficient explanation of his popularity in England. In reality, however, such an explanation is no solution at all, it merely widens the issue ; for we are still left asking for a reason of his continental fame. The problem requires a closer investigation than it has at present received. It was undoubtedly Guevara's *alto estilo* which gave his writings their chief attraction ; and a style so elaborate would only find a reception in a favourable atmosphere, that is among those who had already gone some way towards the creation of a similar style themselves. *A priori* therefore the answer to our question would be that Guevara was no isolated stylist, but only the most famous example of a literary phase, which had its independent representatives all over Europe. A consideration of English prose under the Tudors will, I think, fully confirm this conclusion as far as our own country is concerned, and it will also offer us an explanation, in terms of internal development, of the origin and sources of euphuism.

We have noticed with suspicion that our two translators took their Guevara from the French. And it is therefore quite legitimate to suppose that Berners and North, separated as they were from the original, were as much creators as translators of the euphuistic style. But there are other circumstances connected with Berners, which are much more fatal to Dr Landmann's theory than this. In the first place it appears that the part played by Berners in the history of euphuism has been considerably under-estimated. Mr Sidney Lee was the first to combat the generally accepted view in a criticism

of Mrs Humphry Ward's article on *Euphuism* in the
Encyclopaedia Britannica, in which she follows Dr Landmann. His criticism, which appeared in the *Athenæum*,
was afterwards enlarged in an appendix to his edition
of Berners' translation of *Huon of Bordeaux*. "Lord
Berners' sentences," Mr Lee writes, "are euphuistic
beyond all question; they are characterized by the
forced antitheses, alliteration, and the far-fetched illustrations from natural phenomena, peculiar to Lyly and
his successors[1]." He denies, moreover, that Berners
was any less euphuistic than North, and gives parallel
extracts from their translations to prove this. A comparison of the two passages in question can leave no
doubt that Mr Lee's deduction is correct. Mr Bond
therefore is in grave error when he writes, "North
endeavoured what Berners had not aimed at, to reproduce in his Diall the characteristics of Guevara's style,
with the notable addition of an alliteration natural to
English but not to Spanish ; and it is he who must be
regarded as the real founder of our euphuistic literary
fashion[2]." Lyly may indeed have borrowed from North
rather than from Berners; but, if Berners' English was
as euphuistic as North's, and if Berners could show
fourteen editions to North's two before 1580, it is
Berners and not North who must be described as "the
real founder of our euphuistic literary fashion." And
as Mr Lee shows, his nephew Sir Francis Bryan must
share the title with him, for the colophon of the *Golden
Boke* states that the translation was undertaken "at the
instaunt desire of his nevewe Sir Francis Bryan Knyghte."
It was Bryan also who wrote the passage at the
conclusion of the *Boke* applauding the "swete style[3]."

---

[1] Huon of Bordeaux, appendix I., *Lord Berners and Euphuism*, p. 786.
[2] Bond, I. p. 158. [3] See *Athenæum*, July 14, 1883.

This Sir Francis Bryan was a favourite of Henry VIII., a friend of Surrey and Wyatt, possibly of Ascham and of his master Cheke, in fact a very well-known figure at court and in the literary circles of his day[1]. Euphuism must, therefore, have had a considerable vogue even in the days of Henry VIII. If it could be shown that Bryan could read Castilian, the Guevara theory might still possess some plausibility, for it would be argued that Berners learnt his style from his nephew. But, though we know Bryan to have entertained a peculiar affection for Guevara's writings, there is no evidence to prove that he could read them in the original. Indeed when he set himself to translate Guevara's *Dispraise of the life of a courtier*, he, like his uncle, had to go to a French translation[2]. Wherever we turn, in fact, we are met by this French barrier between Guevara and his English translators, which seems to preclude the possibility of his style having exercised the influence ascribed to it by Dr Landmann and those who follow him.

But there is more behind: and we cannot help feeling convinced that the facts we are now about to bring forward ought to dispose of the Landmann-Guevara theory once and for all. In the article before mentioned Mr Lee goes on to say : "The translator's prologue to Lord Berners' *Froissart* written in 1524 and that to be found in other of his works show him to have come under Guevara's or a similar influence before he translated the *Golden Boke*[3]." Here is an extract from the prologue in question. " The most profitable thing in this

---

[1] *Dict. of Nat. Biog.*, Bryan.

[2] The 2nd edition of this book, which was published under another title, is thus described in the B. M. Cat.: "*A looking-glass for the court*...out of Castilian drawne into French by A. Alaygre ; and out of the French into English by Sir F. Briant."

[3] Huon, p. 787.

world for the institution of the human life is history. Once the continual reading thereof maketh young men equal in prudence to old men, and to old fathers striken in age it ministereth experience of things. More it yieldeth private persons worthy of dignity, rule and governance: it compelleth the emperors, high rulers, and governors to do noble deeds to the end they may obtain immortal glory: it exciteth, moveth and stirreth the strong, hardy warriors, for the great laud that they have after they lie dead, promptly to go in hand with great and hard perils in defence of their country: and it prohibiteth reproveable persons to do mischievous deeds for fear of infamy and shame. So thus through the monuments of writing which is the testimony unto virtue many men have been moved, some to build cities, some to devise and establish laws right, profitable, necessary and behoveful for the human life, some other to find new arts, crafts and sciences, very requisite to the use of mankind. But above all things, whereby man's wealth riseth, special laud and praise ought to be given to history: it is the keeper of such things as have been virtuously done, and the witness of evil deeds, and by the benefit of history all noble, high and virtuous acts be immortal. What moved the strong and fierce Hercules to enterprise in his life so many great incomparable labours and perils? Certainly nought else but that for his great merit immortality might be given him of all folk.... Why moved and stirred Phalerius the King Ptolemy oft and diligently to read books? Forsooth for no other cause but that those things are found written in books that the friends dare not show to the prince[1]." This is of course far from being the full-blown euphuism of Lyly or Pettie, yet we cannot but agree with Mr Lee,

[1] *Froissart*, Globe edition, p. xxviii.

when he declares that "the parallelism of the sentences, the repetition of the same thought differently expressed, the rhetorical question, the accumulation of synonyms, the classical references, are irrefutable witnesses to the presence of euphuism[1]." But Mr Lee appeared to be quite unconscious of the full significance of his discovery. *It means that Berners was writing euphuism in* 1524, *five years before Guevara published his book in Spain.* No critic, as far as I have been able to discover, has shown any consciousness of this significant fact[2], which is of course of the utmost importance in this connexion; as, if it is to carry all the weight that is at first sight due to it, the theory that euphuism was a mere borrowing from the Spanish must be pronounced entirely exploded. But it is as well not to be over-confident. Guevara's *Libro Aureo,* his earliest work, was undoubtedly first published by his authority in 1529, but there seems to be a general feeling that the book had previously appeared in pirated form. This feeling is based upon the title of the 1529 edition[3], which describes the book as "*nueua-mente reuisto por su señoria,*" and upon certain remarks of Hallam in his *Literature of Europe.* Though I can find no confirmation for the statements he makes upon the authority of a certain Dr West of Dublin, yet the words of so well known a writer cannot be ignored. He quotes Dr West in a footnote as follows : "There are

[1] Huon, p. 788.

[2] After writing the above I have noticed that Mr G. C. Macaulay, in the Introduction to the Globe *Froissart*, writes as follows (p. xvi) : "If nothing else could be adduced to show that the tendency (i.e. euphuism) existed already in English literature, the prefaces to Lord Berners' *Froissart* written before he could possibly have read Guevara, would be enough to prove it."

[3] There are two extant editions of 1529, (i) published at Valladolid, from which the words above are quoted, (ii) published at Enueres, which appears to be an earlier edition. Copies of both in the British Museum.

some circumstances connected with the *Relox* (i.e. the sub-title of the *Libro Aureo*) not generally known, which satisfactorily account for various erroneous statements that have been made on the subject by writers of high authority. The fact is that Guevara, about the year 1518, commenced a life and letters of M. Aurelius which purported to be a translation of a Greek work found in Florence. Having sometime afterwards lent this MS. to the emperor it was surreptitiously copied and printed, as he informs us himself, first in Seville and afterwards in Portugal.... Guevara himself subsequently published it (1529) with considerable additions[1]." From this it appears that previous unauthorised editions of Guevara's book had been published before 1529. Might not Berners therefore have come under Guevara's influence as early as 1524? We must concede that it is possible, but, on the other hand, the difficulties in the way of such a contingency seem almost insuperable. In the first place, if we are to believe Dr West, Guevara did not begin to write his work before 1518, and it was not until "some time afterwards" (whatever this may mean) that it was "surreptitiously copied and printed." It would require a bold man to assert that a book thus published could be influencing the style of an English writer as early as 1524. But further it must be remembered that Berners almost certainly could not read Castilian[2]. Now the earliest known French translation of Guevara is one by Réné Bertaut in 1531, which Berners himself is known to have used[3]. Therefore, if Berners was already under Guevara's influence in 1524, he must have known of an

---

[1] Hallam, *Lit. of Europe*, ed. 1855, vol. I. p. 403 n. Brunet in his *Manuel de Libraire* gives Hallam's view without comment, tome II. "Guevara."

[2] Underhill, p. 69. [3] Bond, vol. I. p. 137.

earlier French pirated translation of an earlier pirated
edition of the *Libro Aureo*. To sum up; if the euphuistic
tendency in English prose is to be ascribed entirely, or
even mainly, to the influence of Guevara's *Libro Aureo*,
we must digest four improbabilities: (i) that there existed
a pirated edition of the book in Spain *earlier* than 1524:
(ii) that this had been translated into French, also before
1524, although the version of Bertaut in 1531 is the
earliest French translation we have any trace of: (iii) that
Berners himself had come across this hypothetical French
edition, again before 1524: and (iv) that the French
translation had so faithfully reproduced the style of the
original, that Berners was able to translate it from French
into English, for the purpose of his prologue to *Froissart*.

In face of these facts, the Guevara theory is no
longer tenable ; and in consequence the whole situation
is reversed, and we approach the problem from the
natural side, the side from which it should have been
approached from the first—that is from the English and
not the Spanish side. I say the natural side, because it
seems to me obvious that the popularity of a foreign
author in any country implies the existence in that
country, previous to the introduction of the author, of
an atmosphere (or more concretely a public) favourable
to the distinguishing characteristics of the author introduced. And so it now appears that Guevara found
favour in England because his style, or something very
like it, was already known there; and it was the most
natural thing in the world that Berners, who shows that
style most prominently, should have been the channel by
which Guevara became known to English readers. The
whole problem of this 16th century prose is analogous to
that of 18th century verse. The solution of both was for
a long time found in foreign influence. It was natural

to assume that France, the pivot of our foreign policy at the end of the 17th century, gave us the classical movement, and that Spain, equally important politically in the 16th century, gave us euphuism. Closer investigation has disproved both these theories[1], showing that, while foreign influence was undoubtedly an immense factor in the *development* of these literary fashions, their real *origin* was English.

The proof of this does not rest entirely on the case of Berners. We might even concede that he was acquainted with an earlier edition of Guevara, and that his style was actually derived from Spanish sources, without surrendering our thesis that euphuism was a natural growth. Berners' euphuism, whatever its origin, was premature; and, though the *Golden Boke* passed through twelve editions between 1534 and 1560, we cannot say that its style influenced English writing until the time of Lyly, for its vogue was confined to a small class of readers, designated by Mr Underhill as the "Guevara-group." On the other hand, it is possible to trace a feeling towards euphuism among writers who were quite outside this group.

Latimer, for example, delighted in alliterative turns of speech, though the antithetical mannerisms are absent in him. His famous denunciation of the unpreaching prelates is an excellent instance:

"But now for the faults of unpreaching prelates, methink I could guess what might be said for the excusing of them. They are so troubled with lordly living, they be so placed in palaces, couched in courts, ruffling in their rents, dancing in their dominions, burdened with ambassages, pampering of their paunches like a monk that maketh his jubilee, munching in their mangers, and

---

[1] For 18th century v. Gosse, *From Shakespeare to Pope*.

moiling in their gay manors and mansions, and so troubled with loitering in their lordships, that they cannot attend it."

Here is no transverse alliteration, such as we find so frequently in Lyly, but a simple alliteration—"a rudimentary euphuism of balanced and alliterative phrases, probably like the alliteration of Anglo-Saxon homilies, borrowed from popular poetry[1]." Latimer also employs the responsive method so frequently used by Lyly. "But ye say it is new learning. Now I tell you it is old learning. Yea, ye say, it is old heresy new scoured. Nay, I tell you it is old truth long rusted with your canker, and now made new bright and scoured." It is no long step from this to the rhetorical question and its formal answer "ay but——." Alliteration is not found in Guevara; it was an addition, and a very important one, made by his translators. This was at any rate a purely native product, and cannot be assigned to Spain. The antithesis and parallelism were the fruits of humanism, and they appear, combined with Latimer's alliteration, in the writings of Sir John Cheke and his pupil Roger Ascham. Cheke's famous criticism of Sallust's style, as being "more art than nature and more labour than art," introduces us at once to euphuism, and gives us by the way a very excellent comment upon it. Again he speaks of "magistrates more ready to tender all justice and pitifull in hearing the poor man's causes which ought to amend matters more than you can devise and were ready to redress them better than you can imagine[2]"; which is a good example of the euphuistic combination of alliteration and balance.

In Ascham the style is still more marked. There are, indeed, so many examples of euphuism in the

[1] Craik, vol. I. p. 224.   [2] Craik, p. 258.

Schoolmaster and in the *Toxophilus*, that one can only select. As an illustration of transverse alliteration quite as complex as any in *Euphues*, we may notice the following : " Hard wittes be hard to receive, but sure to keep; painfull without weariness, hedefull without wavering, constant without any new fanglednesse ; bearing heavie things, though not lightlie, yet willinglie ; entering hard things though not easily, yet depelie[1]." Classical allusions abound throughout Ascham's work, and he occasionally indulges in the ethics of natural history as follows :

" Young Graftes grow not onlie sonest, but also fairest and bring always forth the best and sweetest fruite ; young whelps learne easilie to carrie ; young Popingeis learne quickly to speak ; and so, to be short, if in all other things though they lacke reason, sense, and life, the similitude of youth is fittest to all goodnesse, surelie nature in mankinde is more beneficial and effectual in this behalfe[2]."

We know that Lyly had read the *Schoolmaster*, as he took the very title of his book from its description of Εὐφυής as " he that is apte by goodnesse of witte and applicable by readiness of will to learning "—a description which is in itself a euphuism ; and it is probable that he knew his Ascham as thoroughly as he did his Guevara.

Sir Henry Craik has some very pertinent remarks on the peculiarities of Ascham's style. "One of these," he writes, "is his proneness to alliteration, due perhaps to his desire to reproduce the most striking features of the Early English......A tendency of an almost directly opposite kind is the balance of sentences which he imitates from Classical models......These two are

---

[1] Arber, *Schoolmaster*, p. 35.　　　　[2] *id.*, p. 46.

perhaps the most striking characteristics of Ascham's prose; and it is interesting to observe how much the structure of the sentence in the more elaborated stages of English prose is due to their combination[1]." Here we have the two elements of our native-grown euphuism, and their origins, carefully distinguished. Of course with euphuism we do not commence English prose; that is already centuries old; but we are dealing with the beginnings of English prose style, by which we mean a conscious and artistic striving after literary effect. That the first stylists should look to the rhetoricians for their models was inevitable, and of these there were two kinds available; the classical orators and the alliterative homilies of the Early English. But, deferring this point for a later treatment, let us conclude our study of the evolution of euphuism in England.

So far we have been dealing with euphuistic tendencies only, since in the style of Ascham and his predecessors, alliteration and antithesis are not employed consistently, but merely on occasion for the sake of emphasis. Other marks of euphuism, such as the fantastic embroidery of mythical beasts and flowers, are absent. Even in North's *Diall* alliteration is not profuse, and similes from natural history are comparatively rare. In George Pettie, however, we find a complete euphuist before *Euphues*. This writer again brings us in touch with that Oxford atmosphere, which, I maintain, surrounded the birth of the full-blown euphuism. A student of Christ Church, he took his B.A. degree in 1569[2], and so probably just escaped being a contemporary of Lyly. But, as he was a "dear friend" of William Gager, who was a considerably younger man than himself, it seems probable that he continued his Oxford connexion after his degree.

[1] Craik, I. p. 269.   [2] *Dict. of Nat. Biog.*, Pettie.

However this may be, he published his *Petite Pallace of Pettie his Pleasure*, which so exactly anticipates the style of *Euphues*, in 1576, only two years before the later book. The *Petite Pallace* was an imitation of the famous *Palace of Pleasure* published in 1566 by William Painter, who, though he had known Guevara's writings, drew his material almost entirely from Italian sources. That Pettie also possessed a knowledge of Spanish literature, as we should expect from the period of his residence at Oxford, is shown by his translation of Guazzo's *Civile Conversation* in 1581, to which he affixes a euphuistic preface. This again was only a left-handed transcript from the French. Therefore the Spanish elements, though undoubtedly present, cannot be insisted upon. We may concede that Pettie had read North, or even go so far as to assert with Mr Underhill that he was acquainted with "parts of the Gallicized Guevara," without lending countenance to Dr Landmann's radical theories. No one, reading the *Petite Pleasure*, can doubt that Pettie was the real creator of euphuism in its fullest development, and that Lyly was only an imitator. Though I have already somewhat overburdened this chapter, I cannot refrain from quoting a passage from Pettie, not only as an example of his style, but also because the passage is in itself so delightful, that it is one's duty to rescue it from oblivion:

"As amongst all the bonds of benevolence and good will, there is none more honourable, ancient, or honest than marriage, so in my fancy there is none that doth more firmly fasten and inseparably unite us together than the same estate doth, or wherein the fruits of true friendship do more plenteously appear: in the father is a certain severe love and careful goodwill towards the child, the child beareth a fearful affection and awful obedience towards the father: the master hath an imperious regard of the servant, the servant a servile care of the master. The friendship amongst men is grounded upon no love and dissolved upon every light occasion: the goodwill of kinsfolk is constantly cold, as much of custom as of devotion: but in this stately estate of matrimony there is nothing fearful, all things are done faithfully without doubting, truly without doubling, willingly without constraint, joyfully without complaint: yea there is such a general consent and mutual agreement between the man and wife, that they both wish and will covet and crave one thing. And as a scion grafted in a strange stalk, their natures being united by growth, they become one and together bear one fruit: so the love of the wife planted in the breast of her husband, their hearts by continuance of love become one, one sense and one soul serveth them both. And as the scion severed from the stock withereth away, if it be not grafted in some other: so a loving wife separated from the society of her husband withereth away in woe and leadeth a life no less pleasant than death[1]." Lyly never wrote anything to equal this. Indeed it is not unworthy of the lips of one of Shakespeare's heroines.

The euphuism of the foregoing quotation will be readily detected. The sole difference between the styles of Lyly and Pettie is that, while Pettie's similes from nature are simple and natural, Lyly, with his knowledge of Pliny and of the bestiaries, added his fabulous "unnatural natural history." Pettie's book was popular for the time, three editions of it being called for in the first year of its publication, but it was soon to be thrust aside by the fame of the much more pretentious, and,

---

[1] I have taken the liberty of modernising the spelling.

apart from the style, better constructed *Euphues* of Lyly.
In truth, as Gabriel Harvey justly but unkindly remarks,
"Young Euphues but hatched the eggs his elder freendes
laid." But the parental responsibility and merit must
be attributed to him who hatches. It was Lyly who
made euphuism famous and therefore a power; and,
despite the fact that he marks the culmination of the
movement, he is the most dynamical of all the euphuists.

It remains to sum up our conclusions respecting the
origin and development of this literary phase. Difficult
as it is to unravel the tangled network of obscure
influences which surrounded its birth, I venture to think
that a sufficiently complete disproof of that extreme
theory, which would ascribe it entirely to Guevara's
influence, has been offered. Guevara, in the translation
of Berners, undoubtedly took the field early, but, as we
have seen, Berners was probably feeling towards the
style before he knew Guevara; and moreover the bishop's
alto estilo must have suffered considerably while passing
through the French. Even allowing everything, as we
have done, for the close connexion between Spain and
England, for the Spanish tradition at Oxford, and for the
interest in peninsular writings shown by Lyly's immediate
circle of friends, we cannot accord to Dr Landmann's
explanation anything more than a very modified acceptance. Nor would a complete rejection of this solution
of the Lyly problem render English euphuism inex-
plicable ; for something very like it would naturally
have resulted from the close application of classical
methods to prose writing ; and in the case of Cheke and
Ascham we actually see the process at work. And yet
Lyly owed a great debt to Guevara. A true solution,
therefore, must find a place for foreign as well as native
influences. And to say that the Spanish intervention

confirmed and hastened a development already at work, of which the original impulse was English, is, I think, to give a due allowance to both.

SECTION III. *Lyly's Legatees and the relation between Euphuism and the Renaissance.*

The publication of *Euphues* was the culmination, rather than the origin, of that literary phase to which it gave its name. And the vogue of euphuism after 1579 was short, lasting indeed only until about 1590; yet during these ten years its influence was far-reaching, and left a definite mark upon later English prose. It would be idle, if not impossible, to trace its effects upon every individual writer who fell under its immediate fascination. Moreover the task has already been performed in a great measure by M. Jusserand[1] and Mr Bond[2]. They have shown once and for all that Greene, Lodge, Welbanke, Munday, Warner, Wilkinson, and above all Shakespeare, were indebted to our author for certain mannerisms of style. I shall therefore content myself with noticing two or three writers, tainted with euphuism, who have been generally overlooked, and who seem to me important enough, either in themselves, or as throwing light upon the subject of the essay. to receive attention.

The first of these is the dramatist Kyd, who completed his well-known *Spanish Tragedy* between 1584 and 1589, that is at the height of the euphuistic fashion. This play was apparently an inexhaustible joke to the Elizabethans; for the references to it in later dramatists are innumerable. One passage must have been particularly famous, for we find it parodied most elaborately by

---

[1] Jusserand, ch. IV.   [2] Bond, vol. I. pp. 164–175.

Field, as late as 1606, in his *A Woman is a Weathercock*[1].
The passage in question, which was obviously inspired by
Lyly, runs as follows :

> " Yet might she love me for my valiance:
> I, but that's slandered by captivity.
> Yet might she love me to content her sire:
> I, but her reason masters her desire.
> Yet might she love me as her brother's friend:
> I, but her hopes aim at some other end.
> Yet might she love me to uprear her state:
> I, but perhaps she loves some nobler mate.
> Yet might she love me as her beautie's thrall:
> I, but I feare she cannot love at all."

Nathaniel Field's parody of this melodramatic nonsense
is so amusing that I cannot forbear quoting it. This
time the despairing lover is Sir Abraham Ninny, who
quotes Kyd to his companions, and they with the cry of
" Ha God-a-mercy, old Hieromino ! " begin the game of
parody, which must have been keenly enjoyed by the
audience. Field improves on the original by putting the
alternate lines of despair into the mouths of Ninny's
jesting friends. It runs, therefore :

> " —Yet might she love me for my lovely eyes.
> —Ay but, perhaps your nose she does despise.
> —Yet might she love me for my dimpled chin.
> —Ay but, she sees your beard is very thin.
> —Yet might she love me for my proper body.
> —Ay but, she thinks you are an arrant noddy.
> —Yet might she love me 'cause I am an heir.
> —Ay but, perhaps she does not like your ware.
> —Yet might she love me in despite of all.
> (the lady herself)—Ay but indeed I cannot love at all."

This parody, apart from any interest it possesses for the
student of Lyly, is an excellent illustration of the ways
of Elizabethan playwrights, and of the thorough knowledge of previous plays they assumed their audience to

[1] Act I. Sc. II.

have possessed. There are several other examples of Kyd's acquaintance with the *Euphues* in the *Spanish Tragedy*[1], in the other dramas[2], and in his prose works[3], which it is not necessary to quote. But there is one more passage, again from his most famous play, which is so full of interest that it cannot be passed over in silence. It is a counsel of hope to the despairing lover, and assumes this inspiring form:

> "My Lord, though Belimperia seem thus coy
> Let reason hold you in your wonted joy;
> In time the savage Bull sustains the yoke,
> In time all Haggard Hawkes will stoop to ιure,
> In time small wedges cleave the hardest Oake,
> In time the flint is pearst with softest shower,
> And she in time will fall from her disdain,
> And rue the sufferance of your deadly paine[4]."

Now these lines are practically a transcript of the opening words of the 47th sonnet in Watson's *Hekatompathia* published in 1582. Remembering Lyly's penetrating observation that "the soft droppes of rain pearce the hard marble, many strokes overthrow the tallest oake[5]," and bearing in mind that the high priest of euphuism himself contributed a commendatory epistle to the *Hekatompathia*, we should expect that these Bulls and Hawkes and Oakes were choice flowers of speech, culled ιιᴄm that botanico-zoological "garden of prose"—the *Euphues*. But as a matter of fact Watson himself informs us in a note that his sonnet is an imitation of the Italian Serafino, from whom he also borrows other sonnet-conceits in the same volume, some of which are full of similar references to the properties of animals and

---

[1] *Sp. Trag.*, Act IV. 190 (cp. *Euphues*, p. 146).

[2] *Soliman and Perseda*, Act III. 130 (cp. *Euphues*, p. 100), and Aᴂt II. 199.

[3] *Kyd's Works* (Boas), p. 288, and ch. IX.

[4] *Sp. Trag.* Act II. 1–8.   [5] *Euphues*, p. 337.

plants. The conclusion is forced upon us therefore that Watson and Lyly went to the same source, or, if a knowledge of Italian cannot be granted to our author, that he borrowed from Watson. At any rate Watson cannot be placed amongst the imitators of *Euphues*. Like Pettie and Gosson he must share with Lyly the credit of creation. He was a friend of Lyly's at Oxford; they dedicated their books to the same patron, and they employed the same publisher. Moreover, the little we have of Watson's prose is highly euphuistic, and it is apparent from the epistle above mentioned that he was on terms of closest intimacy with the author of *Euphues*. In him we have another member of that interesting circle of Oxford euphuists, who continued their connexion in London under de Vere's patronage.

Watson again was a friend of the well-known poet Richard Barnefield, who though too young in 1578 to have been of the University coterie of euphuists, shows definite traces of their affectation in his works. The conventional illustrations from an "unnatural natural history" abound in his *Affectionate Shepherd*[1] (1594), and he repeats the jargon about marble and showers: which we have seen in Lyly, Watson and Kyd. Again in his *Cynthia* (1594) there is a distinct reference to the opening words of *Euphues* in the lines,

> "Wit without wealth is bad, yet counted good ;
> Wealth wanting wisdom's worse, yet deemed as well[3]."

His prose introduction betrays the same influence.

These then are a few among the countless scribblers of those prolific times who fell under the spell of the euphuistic fashion. They are mentioned, either because their connexion with the movement has been over-

---

[1] *Poems*, Arber, pp. 18 and 19.   [2] *id.*, p. 24.
[3] *id.*, p. 51.

looked, or because they throw a new and important light upon Lyly himself. Of other legatees it is impossible to treat here ; and it is enough, without tracing it in any detail, to indicate "the slender euphuistic thread that runs in iron through Marlowe, in silver through Shakespeare, in bronze through Bacon, in more or less inferior metal through every writer of that age[1]."

There is nothing strange in this infatuation, if we remember that euphuism was "the English type of an all but universal disease[2]," as Symonds puts it. Dr Landmann, we have decided, was wrong in his insistence upon foreign influence ; but his error was a natural one, and points to a fact which no student of Renaissance literature can afford to neglect. Matthew Arnold long ago laid down the clarifying principle that "the criticism which alone can much help us for the future, is a criticism which regards Europe as being, for intellectual and spiritual purposes, one great confederation, bound to a joint action and working to a common result[3]." And the truth of this becomes more and more indisputable, the longer we study European history, whether it be from the side of Politics, of Religion, or of Art. Landmann ascribes euphuism to Spain, Symonds ascribes it to Italy, and an equally good case might be made out in favour of France. There is truth in all these hypotheses, but each misses the true significance of the matter, which is that euphuism must have come, and would have come, without any question of borrowing.

The date 1453 is usually taken as a convenient starting point for the Renaissance, though the movement was already at work in Italy, for that was the year of

[1] Symonds, p. 407.   [2] *id.*, p. 404.
[3] *Essays in Criticism*, I. p. 39.

Byzantium's fall and of the diffusion of the classics over Europe. But, for the countries outside Italy, I think that the date 1493 is almost as important. Hitherto the new learning had been in a great measure confined to Italy, but with the invasion of Charles VIII., which commences a long period of French and Spanish occupation of Italian soil, the Renaissance, especially on its artistic side, began to find its way into the neighbouring states, and through them into England. It is the old story, so familiar to sociologists, of a lower civilization falling under the spell of the culture exhibited by a more advanced subject population, of a conqueror worshipping the gods of the conquered. It is the story of the conquest of Greece by Rome, of the conquest of Rome by the Germans. But the interesting point to notice is that, when the "barbarian" Frenchman descended from the Alps upon the fair plains of Lombardy, the Italian Renaissance was already showing signs of decadence. It was in the age of the Petrarchisti, of Aretino, of Doni, and of Marini that Europe awoke to the full consciousness of the wonders of Italian literature. Thus it was that those beyond the Alps drank of water already tainted. That France, Spain, and England should be attracted by the affectations of Italy, rather than by what was best in her literature, was only to be expected. "It was easier to catch the trick of an Aretino, and a Marini, than to emulate the style of a Tasso or a Castiglione" : and besides they were themselves inventing similar extravagances independently of Italy. The purely formal ideal of Art had in Spain already found expression among the courtiers of Juan II. of Castile. One of them, Baena, writes as follows of poetry : " that it cannot be learned or well and properly known, save by the man of very deep and subtle invention, and of a very

lofty and fine discretion, and of a very healthy and un-
erring judgment, and such a one must have seen and
heard and read many and diverse books and writings,
and know all languages and have frequented kings'
Courts and associated with great men and beheld and
taken part in worldly affairs; and finally he must be of
gentle birth, courteous and sedate, polished, humorous,
polite, witty, and have in his composition honey, and
sugar, and salt, and a good presence and a witty manner
of reasoning; moreover he must be also a lover and ever
make a show and pretence of it [1]." Such a catalogue of
the poet's requisites might have been written by any
one of our Oxford euphuists; and Watson, at least,
among them fulfilled all its conditions.

The Italian influence, therefore, did but hasten a
process already at work. The reasons for this universal
movement are very difficult to determine. But among
many suggestions of more or less value, a few causes of
the change may here be hazarded. In the first place,
then, the Renaissance happened to be contemporaneous
with the death of feudalism. The ideal of chivalry is
dying out all over Europe; and the romances of chivalry
are everywhere despised. The horizontal class divisions
become obscured by the newly found perpendicular
divisions of nationality; and in Italy and England at
least the old feudal nobility have almost entirely dis-
appeared. A new centre of national life and culture is
therefore in the process of formation, that of the Court;
and thanks to this, the ideal of chivalry gives place to
the new ideal of the courtier or the gentleman. This
ideal found literary expression in the moral Court
treatises, which were so universally popular during the
Renaissance, and of which Guevara, Castiglione, and

---

[1] Butler Clarke, *Spanish Literature*, p. 71.

Lyly are the most famous instances. The ambition of those who frequent Courts has always been to appear distinguished—distinguished that is from the vulgar and the ordinary, or, as we should now say, from the Philistine. In the Courts of the Renaissance period, where learning was considered so admirable, this necessary distinction would naturally take the form of a cultured, if not pedantic, diction; and for this it was natural that men should go to the classics, and more especially to classical orators, as models of good speech. It must not be imagined that this process was a conscious one. In many countries the rhetorical style was already formed by scholars before it became the speech of the Court. In fact the beginnings of modern prose style are to be found in humanism. Ascham with his hatred of the " Italianated gentleman," was probably quite unconscious of his own affinity to that objectionable type, when imitating the style of his favourite Tully in the *Schoolmaster*. The classics it must be remembered were not discovered by the humanists, they were only rediscovered. The middle ages had used them, as they had used the Old Testament, as prophetic books. Virgil's mediaeval reputation for example rests for the most part upon the fourth Eclogue. The humanists, on the other hand, looked upon the classics as literature and valued them for their style. But here again they drank from tainted sources; for, with the exception of a few writers such as Cicero and Terence, the classics they knew and loved best were the product of the silver age of Rome, the characteristics of which are beautifully described by the author of *Marius the Epicurean* in his chapter significantly called *Euphuism*. Few of the Renaissance students had the critical acumen of Cheke, and they fell therefore an easy prey to the stylism of the later Latin writers, with its antithesis and extravagance. But, with all this, men could not quite shake off the middle ages. There is much of the Scholastic in Lyly, and the exuberance of ornament, the fantastic similes from natural history, and the moral lessons deduced from them, are quite mediaeval in feeling. We learnt the lessons of the classics backward; and it was not until centuries after, that men realised that the essence of Hellenism is restraint and harmony.

I have spoken of the movement generally, but it passed through many phases, such as arcadianism, gongorism, dubartism; and yet of all these phases euphuism was, I think, the most important: certainly if we confine our attention to English literature this must be admitted. But, even if we keep our eyes upon the Continent alone, euphuism would seem to be more significant than the movements which succeeded it; for it was a definite attempt, seriously undertaken, to force modern languages into a classical mould, while the other and later affectations were merely passing extravagances, possessing little dynamical importance. In this way, short-lived and abortive as it seemed, euphuism anticipated the literature of the *ancien régime.*

The movement, moreover, was only one aspect of the Renaissance; it was the under-current which in the 18th century became the main stream. Paradoxical as it may seem, the Renaissance in its most modern aspect was a development of the middle ages, and not of the classics. This we call romanticism. As an artistic product it was developed on strictly national and traditional lines, born of the fields as it were, free as a bird and as sweet, giving birth in England to the drama, in Italy to the plastic arts. It is essentially opposed to the classical movement, for it represents the idea as distinct from the form. Lyly

4—2

belongs to both movements, for, while he is the protagonist of the romantic drama, in his *Euphues* we may
discover the source of the artificial stream which, concealed for a while beneath the wild exuberance of the
romantic growth, appears later in the 18th century em-
bracing the whole current of English literature.   Before,
however, proceeding to fix the position of euphuism in
the development of English prose, let us sum up the
results we have obtained from our examination of its
relation to the general European Renaissance.   Origi-
nating in that study of classical style we find so forcibly
advocated by Ascham in his *Schoolmaster*, it was essentially a product of humanism.   In every country scholars
were interested as much in the style as in the matter of
the newly discovered classics.   This was due, partly to
the lateness of the Latin writers chiefly known to them,
partly to the mediaeval preference for words rather than
ideas, and partly to the fact that the times were not yet
ripe for an appreciation of the spirit as distinct from the
letter of the classics.   In Italy, in France, and in Spain,
therefore, we may find parallels to euphuism without
supposing any international borrowings.   *Euphues*, in
fact, is not so much a reflection of, as a *Glasse for
Europe*.

SECTION IV.   *The position of Euphuism in the history
of English prose.*

A few words remain to be said about this literary
curiosity, by way of assigning a place to it in the history
of our prose.   To do so with any scientific precision is
impossible, but there are many points of no small
significance in this connexion, which should not be
passed over.

English prose at the beginning of the 16th century, that is before the new learning had become a power in the land, though it had not yet been employed for artistic purposes, was already an important part of our literature, and possessed a quality which no national prose had exhibited since the days of Greece, the quality of popularity[1]. This popularity, which arose from the fact that French and Latin had for so long been the language of the ruling section of the community, is still the distinction which marks off our prose from that of other nations. In Italy, for example, the language of literature is practically incomprehensible to the dwellers on the soil. But what English prose has gained in breadth and comprehension by representing the tongue of the people, it has lost in subtlety. French prose, which developed from the speech of the Court, is a delicate instrument, capable of expressing the finest shades of meaning, while the styles of George Meredith and of Henry James show how difficult it is for a subtle intellect to move freely within the limitations of English prose. Indeed, "it is a remarkable fact," as Sainte Beuve noticed, "and an inversion of what is true of other languages that, in French, prose has always had the precedence over poetry." Repeated attempts, however, have been made to capture our language, and to transport it into aristocratic atmospheres; and of these attempts the first is associated with the name of Lyly.

We have seen that English euphuism was at first a flower of unconscious growth sprung from the soil of humanism. But ultimately, in the hands of Pettie, Gosson, Lyly, and Watson, it became the instrument of an Oxford coterie deliberately and consciously employed for the purpose of altering the form of English

[1] Cf. Earle, pp. 422, 423.

prose. These men did not despise their native tongue; they used the purest English, carefully avoiding the favourite "ink-horn terms" of their contemporaries: they admired it, as one admires a wild bird of the fields, which one wishes to capture in order to make it hop and sing in a golden cage. The humanists were already developing a learned style within the native language; Lyly and his friends utilized this learned style for the creation of an aristocratic type. Euphuism was no "transient phase of madness[1]," as Mr Earle contemptuously calls it, but a brave attempt, and withal a first attempt, to assert that prose writing is an art no less than the writing of poetry; and this alone should give it a claim upon students of English literature.

The first point we must notice, therefore, about English euphuism is that it represents a tendency to confine literature within the limits of the Court—in accordance, one might almost say, with the general centralization of politics and religion under the Tudors —and that, as a necessary result of this, conscious prose style appears for the first time in our language. I say English euphuism, because that is our chief concern, and because though euphuism on the Continent was, as we have seen, the expression in literature of the new ideal of the courtier, yet it was by no means so great an innovation as it was in England, inasmuch as the Romance literatures had always represented the aristocracy. The form which this style assumed was dependent upon the circumstances which gave it birth, and upon the general conditions of the age. Owing to the former it became erudite, polished, precise, meet indeed for the "parleyings" of courtiers and maids-in-waiting; but it was to the latter that it owed its essentials. Hitherto we have contented

[1] Earle, p. 436.

ourselves with indicating the rhetorical aspect of euphuism. We have seen that the Latin orators and the writers of our English homilies exercised a considerable influence over the new stylists. It was natural that rhetoricians should attract those who were desirous of writing ornamental and artistic prose, and one feels inclined to believe that it was not entirely for spiritual reasons that Lyly frequently attended Dr Andrews' sermons[1]. But the euphuistic manner has a wider significance than this, for it marks the transition from poetry to prose.

"The age of Elizabeth is pre-eminently an age of poetry, of which prose may be regarded as merely the overflow[2]." It was at once the end of the mediaeval, and the beginning of the modern, world, and consequently, it displays the qualities of both. But the future lay with the small men rather than with the great. Shakespeare and Milton were no innovators. With their names the epoch of primitive literature, which finds expression in the drama and the epic, ends, while it reaches its highest flights. The dawn of the modern epoch, the age of prose and of the novel, is, on the other hand, connected with the names of Lyly, Sidney, and Nash. Thus, as in the 18th century poetry was subservient, and so became assimilated, to prose, so the prose of the 16th century exhibited many of the characteristics of verse. And of this general literary feature euphuism is the most conspicuous example; for in its employment of alliteration and antithesis, in addition to the excessive use of illustration and simile which characterizes arcadianism and its successors, the style of Lyly is transitional in structure as well as in ornament. Moreover the alliteration, which is peculiar to English euphuism,

[1] Bond, I. p. 60.   [2] Raleigh, p. 45.

gives it a musical element which its continental parallels lacked. The dividing line between alliteration and rhyme, and between antithesis and rhythm, is not a broad one[1]. Indeed Pettie found it so narrow that he occasionally lapsed into metrical rhythm. And so, though we cannot say that euphuism is verse, we can say that it partakes of the nature of verse. In this endeavour to provide an adequate structure for the support of the mass of imagery that the taste of the age demanded, it showed itself superior to the rival prose fashions. *Euphues* is a model of form beside the tedious prolixity of the *Arcadia,* or the chaotic effusions of Nash. The weariness, which the modern reader feels for the romance of Lyly, is due rather to the excessive quantity of its metaphor, which was the fault of the age, than to its pedantic style.

I write loosely of " style," but strictly speaking the euphuists paid especial attention to diction. And here again the poetical and aristocratic tendencies of euphuism show themselves. For diction, which is the art of selection, the selection of apt words, is of course one of the first essentials of poetic art, and is also more prominent in the prose of Court literature than elsewhere. The precision, the *finesse,* the subtlety, of French prose has only been attained by centuries of attention to diction. English prose, on the other hand, is singularly lacking in this quality ; and for this cause it would never have produced a Flaubert, despite its splendid achievements in style. Had euphuism been more successful, it might have altered the whole aspect of later English prose, by giving us in the 16th century that

---

[1] This touches upon the famous dispute between Dr Schwan and Dr Goodlet which is excellently dealt with by Mr Child, p. 77.

quality of diction which did not become prominent in our prose until the days of Pater and the purists.

And yet, though it failed in this particular, the influence of the general qualities of its style upon later prose must have been incalculable. The vogue of euphuism as a craze was brief; but *Euphues* received fresh publication about once every three years down to 1636, and long after its social popularity had become a thing of the past, it probably attracted the careful study of those who wished to write artistic prose. The only model of prose form which the age possessed could scarcely sink into oblivion, or become out of date, until its principal lessons had been so well learnt as to pass into common-places. The exaggerations, which first gave it fame, were probably discounted by the more sincere appreciation of later critics, to whom its more sterling qualities would appeal. For some reason, the musical properties of euphuism do not appear to have found favour among those critics, and this was probably a loss to our literature. "Alliteration," as Professor Raleigh remarks, "is often condemned as a flaw in rhymed verse, and it may well be open to question whether Lyly did not give it its true position in attempting to invent a place for it in what is called prose[1]." Possibly its failure in this respect was due to the growth of that intellectual asceticism, and that reaction against the domination of poetry, which are, I think, intimately bound up with the fortunes of Puritanism. The beginning of this reaction is visible as early as 1589 in the words of Warner's preface to *Albion's England*, which display the very affectation they protest against: "onely this error may be thought hatching in our English, that to runne on the letter we often runne from the matter:

[1] Raleigh, p. 47.

and being over prodigall in similes we become lesse profitable in sentences and more prolixious to sense." But, however this may be, it was the formal rather than the musical qualities which gave *Euphues* its dynamical importance in the history of English prose. Subsequent writers had much to learn from a book in which the principle of design is for the first time visible. With euphuism, antithesis and the use of balanced sentences came to stay. We may see them in the style of Johnson and Gibbon, while alliterative antithesis reappears to-day in the shape of the epigram. Doubtless Lyly abused the antithetical device; but his successors had only to discover a means of skilfully concealing the structure, an improvement which the early euphuists, with all the enthusiasm of inventors, could not have appreciated.

Moreover, in aiming at elegance and precision, Lyly attained a lucidity almost unequalled among his contemporaries. His attention to form saved him from the besetting sin of Elizabethan prose,—incoherence by reason of an overwhelming display of ornament. His very illustrations were subject to the restraint which his style demanded, being sown, to use his own metaphor, "here and there lyke Strawberries, not in heapes, lyke Hoppes[1]." Arcadianism came as a reaction against euphuism, attempting to replace its artificiality by simplicity. But how infinitely more preferable is the novel of Lyly, with its artificial precision and lucidity, to the conscious artlessness of Sidney's *Arcadia*, with its interminable sentences and confused syntax. As a modern euphuist has taught us, of all poses the natural pose is the most irritating. In accordance with his desire for precision, Lyly made frequent use of the short sentence. In this we have another indication of his

[1] *Euphues*, p. 220.

modernity: for the short sentence, which is so characteristic of English prose style to-day, occurs more often in
his work than in the writings of any of his predecessors.
And, in reference to the same question of lucidity, we
may notice that he was the first writer who gave special
attention to the separation of his prose into paragraphs,—
a matter apparently trivial, but really of no small
importance. Finally, it is a remarkable fact that the
number of words to be found in *Euphues* which have
since become obsolete is a very small one—"at most but
a small fraction of one per cent.[1]" And this is in itself
sufficient to indicate the influence which Lyly's novel
has exerted upon English prose. As he reads it, no one
can avoid being struck by the modernity of its language,
an impression not to be obtained from a perusal of the
plays. The explanation is simple enough. The plays
were not read or absorbed by their author's contemporaries and successors; *Euphues* was. In the domain
of style, *Euphues* was dynamical; the plays were not.

But the true value of Lyly's prose lies not so much
in what it achieved as in what it attempted; for the
qualities, which euphuism, by its insistence upon design
and elegance, really aimed at, were strength, brilliancy
and refinement. For the first time in the history of our
literature, men are found to write prose with the purpose
of fascinating and enticing the reader, not merely by
what is said, but also by the manner of saying it.
"Lyly" (and, we may add, his associates), writes his latest
editor, "grasped the fact that in prose no less than in
poetry, the reader demanded to be led onward by a
succession of half imperceptible shocks of pleasure in
the beauty and vigour of diction, or in the ingenuity
of phrasing, in sentence after sentence—pleasure in-

[1] Child, p. 41.

separable from that caused by a perception of the nice adaptation of words to thought, pleasure quite other than that derivable from the acquisition of fresh knowledge[1]." The direct influence of the man who first taught us this lesson, who showed us that a writer, to be successful, should seek not merely to express himself, but also to study the mind of his reader, must have been something quite beyond computation. And that his direct influence was not more lasting was due, in the first place, to the fact that he had not grasped the full significance of this psychological aspect of style, if we may so call it, which he and his friends had been the first to discover. As with most first attempts, euphuism, while bestowing immense benefits upon those who came after, was itself a failure. The euphuists perceived the problem of style, but successfully attacked only one half of it. More acute than their contemporaries, they realised the principle of economy, but, as with one who makes an entirely new mechanical invention, they were themselves unable to appreciate what their discovery would lead to. They were right in addressing themselves to the task of attracting, and stimulating, the reader by means of precision, pointed antithesis, and such like attempts to induce pleasurable mental sensations, but they forgot that anyone must eventually grow weary under the influence of continuous excitation without variation. The soft drops of rain pierce the hard marble, many strokes overthrow the tallest oak, and much monotony will tire the readiest reader. Or, to use the phraseology of a somewhat more recent scientist, they "considered only those causes of force in language which depend upon economy of the mental *energies*," they paid no attention to "those which depend upon the economy

---

[1] Bond, I. p. 146.

of the mental *sensibilities*[1]." This is one explanation
of the weariness with which *Euphues* fills the modern
reader, and of the speed with which, in spite of its
priceless pioneer work, that book was superseded and
forgotten in its own days. It is our duty to give it its
full meed of recognition, but we can understand and
forgive the ungratefulness of its contemporaries.

Another cause of the oblivion which so soon overtook the famous Elizabethan novel, has already been
suggested. Euphuism was too antagonistic to the
general current of English prose to be successful. Lyly
and his Oxford clique were attempting a revolution
similar to that undertaken, at the same period, by Ronsard and his *Pleiad*. Lyly failed in prose, where Ronsard
succeeded in poetry, because he endeavoured to go back
upon tradition, while the Frenchman worked strictly
within its limits. The attempt to throw Court dress over
the plain homespun of our English prose might have
been attended with success, had our literature been
younger and more easily led astray. As it was, prose in
this country, when euphuism invaded it, could already
show seven centuries of development, and, moreover,
development along the broad and national lines of
common or vulgar speech. Euphuism was after all only
part of the general tendency of the age to focus everything that was good in politics, religion, and art, on the
person and immediate surroundings of the sovereign ;
and the history of the eighteenth century, which saw the
last issue of the series of *Euphues* reprints, is the history
of the collapse of this centralization all along the line,
ending in the complete vindication of the democratic
basis of English life and literature.

With these general remarks we must leave the

[1] H. Spencer, Essays, II. *Phil. of Style.*

subject of euphuism. No history of its origin and its influence can be completely satisfactory : such questions must of necessity receive a speculative and tentative solution, for it is impossible to give them an exact answer which admits of no dispute. The age of Lyly was far more complex than ours, with all our artistic sects and schisms ; the currents of literary influence were multitudinous and extremely involved. As Symonds wrote, " The romantic art of the modern world did not spring like that of Greece from an ungarnered field of flowers. Troubled by reminiscences from the past and by reciprocal influences from one another, the literatures of modern Europe came into existence with composite dialects and obeyed confused canons of taste, exhibited their adolescent vigour with affected graces and showed themselves senile in their cradles." In the field of literature to-day the standards are more numerous, but more distinctive, than those of the Elizabethans. Our ideals are classified with almost scientific exactness, and we wear the labels proudly. But the very splendour of the Renaissance was due to the fact that in the same group, in the same artist, were to be found the most diverse ideals and the most opposite methods. They worshipped they knew not what, we know what we worship. Yet this difference does not prevent us from seeing curious points of similarity between our own and those times. The 16th, like the 19th century, was a period of revolt from the past : and at such moments men feel a supreme contempt for the common-place in literature. The cry of art for art's sake is raised, and the result is extravagance, euphuism. A wave of intellectual dandyism seems to sweep over the face of literature, aristocratic in its aims and sympathies. Then are the battle lines drawn up, and the spectators watch, with admiration or contempt, the eternally recurrent strife between David and the Philistines; and whether the young hero be clad in the knee-breeches of aestheticism, or the slashed doublet of the courtier; whether he be armed with epigram and sunflower, or with euphuism and camomile; variation of costume cannot conceal the identity of his personality—the personality of the fop of culture.

CHAPTER II.

THE FIRST ENGLISH NOVEL.

DESPITE the disproportionate attention given to euphuism by so many of Lyly's critics, *Euphues* is no less important as a novel than as a piece of prose. We can, however, dismiss this second branch of our subject in fewer words, because the problem of *Euphues* is much simpler and more straightforward than the problem of euphuism. It can scarcely be said that Lyly has yet been thoroughly appreciated as a novelist; indeed, the whole subject of the Elizabethan novel is very far from having received a satisfactory treatment at present. This is not surprising when we consider that the last word remains to be said upon the Elizabethan drama. The birth of modern literature was so sudden, its life, even in the cradle, was so complex that it baffles criticism. Like the peal of an organ with a thousand stops, the English Renaissance seemed to break the stillness of the great mediaeval church, shaking its beautiful sombre walls and filling it from floor to roof with wild, pagan music. Indeed, the more we study those 50 or 60 years which embrace the so-called Elizabethan period, the more are we struck by the fact that, ever since, we have been simply making variations upon the themes which the men of those times gave us. Modern science, modern poetry, modern drama, sat like pages at the feet of the Great Queen. Among these the novel cut but an insignificant figure, although it was the novel which had perhaps the longest future before it. We need not wonder therefore that our first English novelist has been treated by many with neglect. None I think have done more to make amends in this direction than Professor Raleigh and M. Jusserand; the former in his graceful, humorous, and penetrating little book, *The English Novel*; and the latter in his well-known work on *The English Novel in the time of Shakespeare,* which gives one, while reading it, the feeling of being present at a fancy-dress ball, so skilfully does he detect the forms and faces of present-day fiction behind euphuistic mask and beneath arcadian costume. To these two books the present writer owes a debt which all must feel who have stood bewildered upon the threshold of Elizabeth's Court with its glittering throng of genius and wit.

Sudden, however, as was this crop of warriors wielding pen, it must not be forgotten that the dragon's teeth had first been sown in mediaeval soil. With Lyly the English novel came into being, but that child of his genius was not without ancestry or relations. And so, before discussing the character and fortunes of the infant, let us devote a few introductory remarks to pedigree. Roughly speaking, the prose narrative in England, before *Euphues*, falls into three divisions, the romance of chivalry, the *novella*, and the moral Court treatise,—and all three are of foreign extraction, that is to say, they are represented in England by translations only. Chaucer indeed is a mine of material suitable for the novel, but the father of English literature elected to write in verse, and his *Canterbury Tales* have no appreciable influence upon the later prose story. For some reason, the medi-

aeval prose narrative seems to have been confined to the
so-called Celtic races. Certainly, both the romance of
chivalry and the *novella* are to be traced back to French
sources. The *novella*, which, at our period, had become
thoroughly naturalized in Italy, under the auspices of
Boccaccio, had originally sprung from the *fabliaux* of
13th century France. Nor was the *fabliau* the only
article of French production which found a new and
more stimulative home across the Alps ; for just as it is
possible to trace the German Reformation back, through
Huss, to its birth in Wycliff's England, so French critics
have delighted to point out that the Italian Renaissance
itself was but an expansion of an earlier Renaissance in
France, which, for all the strength and maturity it
gained under its new conditions, lost much of that
indescribable flavour of direct simplicity and gracious
sweetness which breathes from the pages of *Aucassin
and Nicolette* and its companion *Amis and Amile.*
Under Charles VIII. and his successors this Renaissance
was carried home, as it were, to die—so subtle is the ebb
and flow of intellectual influences between country and
country. In England the *novella*, of which Chaucer had
made ample use, first appeared in prose dress from the
printing-press of Caxton's successor, Wynkyn de Worde.
The Dutch printer had also published Lord Berners'
translation of *Huon of Bordeaux*, the best romance of
chivalry belonging to the Charlemagne cycle. But,
before the dawn of the 16th century Malory had already
given us *Morte D'Arthur*, from the Arthurian cycle,
printed, as everyone knows, by the industrious Caxton
himself. Thus, if we neglect, as I think we may, translations from the *Gesta Romanorum*, we may say that the
prose narrative appeared in England simultaneously
with the printing-press, a fact which is more than coin-

cidence ; since the multiplication of books, which Caxton began, decreased the necessity for remembering tales ; and therefore it was now possible to dispense with the aid of verse ; in fact Caxton deprived the minstrel of his occupation.

Of the third form of prose narrative—the moral Court treatise—we have already said something. It had appeared in Italy and in Spain, and our connexion with it came from the latter country, through Berners' translation of the *Golden Boke* of Guevara. So slight was the thread of narrative running through this book, that one would imagine at first sight that it could have little to do with the history of our novel. And yet in comparison with its importance in this respect the *novella* and the romance of chivalry are quite insignificant. The two latter never indeed lost their popularity during the Elizabethan age, but they had ceased to be considered respectable—a very different thing—before that age began. The first cause of their fall in the social scale was the disapprobation of the humanists. Ascham, echoing Plato's condemnation of Homer, attacks the romance of chivalry from the moral point of view, at the same time cunningly associating it with " Papistrie." But he holds the *novella* even in greater abhorrence, for, after declaring that the whole pleasure of the *Morte D'Arthur* " standeth in two speciall poyntes, in open mans slaughter, and bold bawdrye," he goes on to say : " and yet ten *Morte Arthurs* do not a tenth part so much harm as one of those bookes, made in Italy and translated in England [1]."

But there were social as well as moral reasons for the depreciation of Malory and Boccaccio. The taste of the age began to find these foreign dishes, if not unpalatable,

[1] *Schoolmaster*, p. 80.

at least not sufficiently delicate. England was fortunate
in receiving the Reformation and the Renaissance at the
same time ; and the men of those " spacious times " set
before their eyes that ideal of the courtier, so exquisitely
embodied by Sir Philip Sidney, in which godliness was
not thought incompatible with refinement of culture and
graciousness of bearing. For the first time our country
became civilized in the full meaning of that word, and
the knight, shedding the armour of barbarism, became
the gentleman, clothed in velvet and silk. The romance
of chivalry, therefore, became old-fashioned ; and it
seemed for a time doomed to destruction until it received
a new lease of life, purged of mediaevalism and modernised by the hands of Sidney himself, under the guise of
arcadianism. While, however, *Arcadia* remained an un-
discovered country, the needs of the age were supplied
by the "moral Court treatise." It was perhaps not so
much that the old stories found little response in the
new form of society, as that they did not reflect that
society. We may well believe that the taste for mirrors,
which now became so fashionable, found its psychological
parallel in the desire of the Elizabethans to discover
their own fashions, their own affectations, themselves,
in the stories they read ; and if this indeed be what is
meant by realism in literature that quality in the novel
dates from those days. In this sense if in no other, in
the sense that he held, for the first time, a polished
mirror before contemporary life and manners, Lyly must
be called the first of English novelists.

The Anatomy of Wit, which it is most important to
distinguish from its sequel, was the descendant in the
direct line from the "moral Court treatise." Something
perhaps of the atmosphere of the *novella* clung about its
pages, but that was only to be expected : Lyly added

incident to the bare scheme of discourses, and for that
he had no other models but the Italians. But Guevara
was his real source. Dr Landmann's verdict, that
"Euphuism is not only adapted from Guevara's *alto
estilo*, but *Euphues* itself, as to its contents, is a mere
imitation of Guevara's enlarged biography of Marcus
Aurelius," has certainly been shown by Mr Bond to be
a gross overstatement; yet there can be no doubt that
the *Diall of Princes* was Lyly's model on the side of
matter, as was Pettie's *Pallace* on the side of style. Our
author's debt to the Spaniard is seen in a correspondence
between many parts of his book and the *Aureo Libro*, in
certain of the concluding letters and discourses, and in
many other ways which Mr Bond has patiently noted[1].
Guevara, however, was but one among many previous
writers to whom Lyly owed obligations. *Euphues* was
justly styled by its author "compiled," being in fact
a mosaic, pieced together from the classics, and especially
Plutarch, Pliny, and Ovid, and from previous English
writers such as Harrison, Heywood, Fortescue, and
Gascoigne; names that indicate the course of literary
"browsing" that Lyly substituted for the ordinary
curriculum at Oxford. To mention all the authors from
whom he borrowed, and to point out the portions of
his novel which are due to their several influences,
would only be to repeat a task already accomplished
by Mr Bond[2].

Allowing for all its author's "picking and stealing,"
The Anatomy of Wit was in the highest sense an original
book; for, though it is the old moral treatise, its form is
new, and it is enlivened by a thin thread of narrative.
The hero Euphues is a young man lately come from
Athens, which is unmistakeably Oxford, to Naples,

[1] Bond, I. pp. 154–156.   [2] Bond, I. pp. 156–159.

which is just as unmistakeably London. Here he soon
becomes the centre of a convivial circle, where he is wise
enough to distinguish between friend and parasite, to
discern the difference between the "faith of Laelius
and the flattery of Aristippus." The story thus opens
bravely, but the words of the title-page, "most necessary
to remember," are ever present in the author's mind,
and before we have reached the fourth page the sermon
is upon us. For "conscience" attired as an old man,
Eubulus, now enters the stage of this Court *morality* and
proceeds to deliver a long harangue upon the folly of
youth, concluding with much excellent though obvious
counsel. We should be in sympathy with the rude
answer of Euphues, were it but curt at the same time,
but, alas, it covers six pages. Having thus imprudently
crushed the "wisdom of eld" by the weight of his
utterance, our hero shows his natural preference for the
companionship and counsel of youth, by forming an
ardent friendship with Philautus, of so close a nature,
that "they used not only one boorde but one bed, one
booke (if so be that they thought it not one too many)."
This alliance, however, is not concluded until Euphues
has given us his own views, together with those of half
antiquity, upon the subject of friendship, or before he
has formally professed his affection in a pompous ad-
dress, beginning "Gentleman and friend," and has been
as formally accepted. By Philautus he is introduced to
Lucilla, the chief female character of the book, a lady,
if we are to believe the description of her "Lilly cheeks
dyed with a Vermilion red," of startling if somewhat
factitious beauty. To say that the plot now thickens
would be to use too coarse a word ; it becomes slightly
tinged with incident, inasmuch as Euphues falls in
love with Lucilla, the destined bride of Philautus. She

reciprocates his passion, and the double fickleness of mistress and friend forms an excellent opportunity, which Lyly does not fail to seize, for infinite moralizings in euphuistic strains. Philautus is naturally indignant at the turn affairs have taken, and the former friends exchange letters of recrimination, in which, however, their embittered feelings are concealed beneath a vast display of classical learning. But Nemesis, swift and sudden, awaits the faithless Euphues. Lucilla, it turns out, is subject to a mild form of erotomania and is constitutionally fickle, so that before her new lover has begun to realise his bliss she has already contracted a passion for some other young gentleman. Thus, struck down in the hour of his pride and passion, Euphues becomes "a changed man," and bethinks himself of his soul, which he has so long neglected. This is the turning-point of the book, the turning-point of half the English novels written since Lyly's day. The remainder of the *Anatomy of Wit* is taken up with what may be described as the private papers of Euphues, consisting of letters, essays, and dialogues, including *A Cooling Carde for all Fond Lovers*, a treatise on education, and a refutation of atheism, and so amid the thunders of the artillery of platitude the first part of *Euphues* closes.

Professor Raleigh's explanation of this tedious moralizing is that Lyly, wit and euphuist, possessed the Nonconformist conscience: " Beneath the courtier's slashed doublet, under his ornate brocade and frills, there stood the Puritan." This I believe to be a mistaken view of the case. As we shall later see reason to suppose, Lyly never became, as did his acquaintance Gosson, a very seriously-minded person. Certainly *Euphues* does not prove that Puritanism was latent in him. The moral atmosphere which pervades it was not of Lyly's invention ; he inherited it from his predecessors Guevara and Castiglione, and he employed it because he knew that it was expected of him. That he moralized not so much from conviction as from convention (to use a euphuism), is, I think, sufficiently proved by the fact that in the second part of his novel, where he is addressing a new public, the pulpit strain is much less frequent, while in his plays it entirely disappears. The *Anatomy of Wit* is essentially the work of an inexperienced writer, feeling his way towards a public, and without sufficient skill or courage to dispense with the conventions which he has inherited from previous writers. One feels, while reading the book, that Lyly was himself conscious that his hero was an insufferable coxcomb, and that he only created him because he wished to comply with the public taste. It may be, as M. Jusserand asserts, that Lyly anticipated Richardson, but, if the light-hearted Oxford madcap had any qualities in common with the sedate bookseller, artistic sincerity was not one of them.

What has just been said is not entirely applicable to the treatise on education which passed under the title of *Euphues and his Ephoebus*. Although simply an adaptation of the *De Educatione* of Plutarch, it was not entirely devoid of originality. Here we find the famous attack upon Oxford, which was, we fear, prompted by a desire to spite the University authorities rather than by any earnest feeling of moral condemnation. But in addition to this there are contributions of Lyly's own invention to the theory of teaching which are not without merit. He was, as we have seen, interested in education. It seems even possible that he had actually practised as a master before the *Euphues* saw light[1]; and, therefore,

[1] Bond, I. p. 10.

we have every reason to suppose that this little treatise was a labour of love. Possibly Ascham's *Schoolmaster* inspired him with the idea of writing it. Certainly, when we have allowed everything for Plutarch's work, enough remains over to justify Mr Quick's inclusion of John Lyly, side by side with Roger Ascham, in his *Educational Reformers*.

But such excellent work has but little to do with the business of novel-writing, and, when we turn to this aspect of the *Anatomy of Wit*, there is little to be said for it from the aesthetic point of view. Indeed, it cannot strictly be called a novel at all. It is the bridge between the moral Court treatise and the novel, and, as such, all its aesthetic defects matter little in comparison with its dynamical value. It was a great step to hang the chestnuts of discourse upon a string of incident. The story is feeble, the plot puerile, but it was something to have a story and a plot which dealt with contemporary life. And lastly, though characterization is not even attempted, yet now and again these euphuistic puppets, distinguishable only by their labels, are inspired with something that is almost life by a phrase or a chance word.

I have said that it is very important to distinguish between the two parts of *Euphues*. Two years only elapsed between their respective publications, but in these two years Lyly, and with him our novel, had made great strides. In 1578 he was not yet a novelist, though the conception of the novel and the capacity for its creation were, as we have just shown, already forming in his brain. In 1580, however, the English novel had ceased to be merely potential; for it had come into being with the appearance of *Euphues and his England*. Here in the same writer, in the same book, and within the space of two years, we may observe one of the most

momentous changes of modern literature in actual process. The *Anatomy of Wit* is still the moral Court
treatise, coloured by the influence of the Italian *novella*;
Euphues and his England is the first English novel.
Lyly unconsciously symbolizes the change he initiated
by laying the scene of his first part in Italy, while in
the second he brings his hero to England. That sea
voyage, which provoked the stomach of Philautus sore,
was an important one for us, since the freight of the
vessel was nothing less than our English novel.

The difference between the two parts is remarkable
in more ways than one, and in none more so than in the
change of dedication. The *Anatomy of Wit*, as was
only fitting in a moral Court treatise, was inscribed to
the gentleman readers; *Euphues and his England*, on the
other hand, made an appeal to a very different class of
readers, and a class which had hitherto been neglected
by authors—"the ladies and gentlewomen of England."
With the instinct, almost, of a religious reformer, Lyly
saw that to succeed he must enlist the ladies on his side.
And the experiment was so successful that I am inclined
to attribute the pre-eminence of Lyly among other
euphuists to this fact alone. "Hatch the egges his
friendes had laid" he certainly did, but he fed the
chicks upon a patent food of his own invention.
Mr Bond suggests that the general attention which the
Anatomy secured by its attacks upon women gave Lyly
the idea for the second part. But, though this was probably the immediate cause of his change of front, something like *Euphues and his England* must have come
sooner or later, because all the conditions were ripe for
its production. Side by side with the ideal of the
courtier had arisen the ideal of the cultured lady.
Ascham, visiting Lady Jane Grey, "founde her in her

chamber reading *Phaedon Platonis* in Greeke and that
with as much delite, as some gentlemen would read a
merie tale in Bocase[1]"; and, when a Queen came to the
throne who could talk Greek at Cambridge, the fashion
of learning for ladies must have received an immense
impetus. With a "blue stocking" showing on the royal
footstool, all the ladies of the Court would at least lay
claim to a certain amount of learning. Dr Landmann
has attributed the vogue of euphuism, at least in part, to
feminine influences, but in so far as England shared that
affectation with the other Courts of Europe, where the
fair sex had not yet acquired such freedom as in England,
we must not press the point too much in this direction.
The importance in English literature of that "monstrous
regiment of women," against which John Knox blew his
rude trumpet so shamelessly, is seen not so much in the
style of *Euphues* as in its contents; indeed, in the second
part of that work euphuism is much less prominent than
in the first. The romance of chivalry and the Italian
tale would be still more distasteful to the new woman
than they were to the new courtier. Doubtless Boccaccio
may have found a place in many a lady's secret book-
shelf as Zola and Guy de Maupassant do perchance to-
day, but he was scarcely suitable for the boudoir table
or for polite literary discussion. Something was needed
which would appeal at once to the feminine taste for
learning and to the desire for delicacy and refinement.
This want was only partially supplied by the moral
Court treatise, which was ostensibly written for the
courtier and not the maid-in-waiting. What was required was a book expressly provided for the eye of
ladies—such a book, in fact, as *Euphues and his England*.
Lyly's discovery of this new literary public and its

---

[1] *Schoolmaster*, p. 47.

requirements was of great importance, for have not the
ladies ever since his day been the patrons and purchasers
of the novel? What would happen to the literary market
to-day were our mothers, wives, and sisters to deny themselves the pleasure of fiction? The very question would
send the blood from Mr Mudie's lips. The two thousand
and odd novels which are published annually in this
country show the existence of a large leisured class in
our community, and this class is undoubtedly the feminine one. The novel, therefore, owes not only its birth,
but its continued existence down to our own day, to the
"ladies and gentlewomen of England"; and this dedication may be taken as a general one for all novels
since Lyly's time. "*Euphues*," he writes, "had rather lye
shut in a Ladye's casket than open in a scholar's studie,"
and he continues, "after dinner you may overlooke him
to keepe you from sleepe, or if you be heavie, to bring
you to sleepe...it were better to hold *Euphues* in your
hands though you let him fall, when you be willing to
winke, then to sowe in a clout, and pricke your fingers
when you begin to nod[1]." "With *Euphues*," remarks
M. Jusserand, "commences in England the literature of
the drawing-room[2]"; and the literature of the drawing-
room is to all intents and purposes the novel.

All the faults of its predecessor are present in *Euphues
and his England*, but they are not so conspicuous. The
euphuistic garb and the mantle of the prophet Guevara
sit more lightly upon our author. In every way his
movements are freer and bolder; having gained con-
fidence by his first success, he now dares to be original.
The story becomes at times quite interesting, even for
a modern reader. At its opening Euphues and Philautus,
who have come to terms on a basis of common con-

---

[1] *Euphues*, p. 220.   [2] Jusserand, p. 5.

demnation of Lucilla, are discovered on their way to
England.   By way of enlivening the weary hours, our
hero, ever ready to play the preacher now that he has
ceased to be the warning, delivers himself of a lengthy,
but highly edifying tale, which evokes the impatient
exclamation of Philautus already quoted ; we may however notice as a sign of progress that Euphues has
substituted a moral narrative for his usual discourse.
The relations between the two friends have become
distinctly amusing, and might, in abler hands, have
resulted in comic situation.   Euphues, having learnt the
lesson of the burnt child, is now a very grave person,
proud of his own experience and of its fruits in himself.
Extremes met,

> " Where pinched ascetic and red sensualist
> Alternately recurrent freeze and burn,"

and it is interesting to note that Euphues embodies
many of the characteristics of the Byronic hero—his
sententiousness, his misogyny, his cynicism born of dis-
illusionment, and his rhetorical flatulency; but he is no
rebel like Manfred because he finds consolation in his
own pre-eminence in a world of platitude.   Conscious
of his dearly bought wisdom, he makes it his continuous
duty, if not pleasure, to rebuke the over-amorous
Philautus, who was at least human, and to enlarge upon
the infidelity of the opposite sex.   Lyly failed to realise
the possibilities of this antagonism of character, because
he always appears to be in sympathy with his hero, and
so misses an opportunity which would have delighted
the heart of Thackeray.   I say "appears," because I
consider that this sympathy was nothing but a pose
which he considered necessary for the popularity of his
book.   It is important however to observe that the idea
of one character as a foil to another, though unde-

veloped, is here present for the first time in our national
prose story.

The tale ended and the voyage over, our friends
arrive in England, where after stopping at Dover " 3 or
4 days, until they had digested ye seas, and recovered
their healths," they proceeded to Canterbury, at which
place they fell in with an old man named Fidus, who
gave them entertainment for body and mind. To those
who have conscientiously read the whole history of
Euphues up to this point, the incident of Fidus will
appear immensely refreshing. It seems to me, in fact,
to mark the highest point of Lyly's skill as a novelist,
doubtless because he is here drawing upon his memory[1]
and not his imagination. The old gentleman, very
different from his prototype Eubulus, moves quite
humanly among his bees and flowers, and tells the
graceful story of his love with a charm that is almost
natural. And, although he checks the action of the
story for thirty-three pages, we are sorry to take leave
of this "fatherlye and friendlye sire"; for he lays for
a time the ghost of homily, which reappears directly
his guests begin to "forme their steppes towards
London." Having reached the Court, in due time
Philautus, in accordance with the prophecies of Euphues
though much to his disgust, falls in love. The lady of
his choice, however, has unfortunately given her heart
to another, by name Surius. The despondent lover,
after applying in vain to an Italian magician for a love-
philtre, at length determines to adopt the bolder line of
writing to his scornful lady. The letter is conveyed in
a pomegranate, and the incident of its presentation is
prettily conceived and displays a certain amount of
dramatic power. The upshot is that Philautus eventually

---

[1] Mr Bond thinks it a picture of Lyly's father.

finds a maiden who is unattached and who is ready to return love for love. Her he marries, and remains behind with "his Violet" in England, while Euphues, less happy than self-satisfied, returns to Athens. The interest of the latter half of the book centres round the house of Lady Flavia, where the principal characters of both sexes meet together and discuss the philosophy of love and the psychology of ladies. Such intellectual gatherings were a recognised institution at Florence at this time, being an imitation of Plato's symposium, and Lyly had already attempted, not so successfully as here, to describe one in the house of Lucilla of the *Anatomy of Wit.*

In every way *Euphues and his England* is an improvement upon its predecessor. The story and plot are still weak, but the situations are often well thought out and treated with dramatic effect. The action indeed is slow, but it moves; and in the story of Fidus it moves comparatively quickly. Such motion of course can scarcely ruffle the mental waters of those accustomed to the breathless whirlwinds which form the heart of George Meredith's novels; but these whirlwinds are as directly traceable to the gentle but fitful agitation of *Euphues*, as was the storm that overtook Ahab's chariot to the little cloud undiscerned by the prophet's eye. The figures, again, that move in Lyly's second novel are no longer clothes filled with moral sawdust. The character of Philautus is especially well drawn, though at times blurred and indistinct. Lyly had not yet passed the stage of creating types, that is of portraying one aspect and an obvious one of such a complex thing as human nature. But a criticism which would be applicable to Dickens is no condemnation of an Elizabethan pioneer. It was much to have attempted characterization, and in the case of Philautus, Iffida, Camilla, and perhaps "the Violet" the attempt was nearly if not quite successful. It is noticeable that for one who was afterwards to become a writer of comedy, Lyly shows a remarkable absence of humour in these novels. Now and again we seem trembling on the brink of humour, when the young wiseacre is brought into contact with his weak-hearted friend, but the line is seldom actually crossed. Wit, as Lyly here understood it, had nothing of the risible in it; for it meant to him little more than a graceful handling of obvious themes.

But the importance of *Euphues* was in its influence, not in its actual achievement. And here again we must reassert the significance of Lyly's appeal to women. "That noble faculty," as Macaulay expresses it, "whereby man is able to live in the past and in the future in the distant and in the unreal," is rarely found in the opposite sex. They delight in novelty, their minds are of a practical cast, and their interests almost invariably lie in the present. The names of Jane Austen, George Eliot, and Mrs Humphry Ward are sufficient to show how entirely successful a woman may be in delineating the life around her. If there is any truth in this generalization, it was no mere coincidence that the first English romance dealing with contemporary life was written expressly for the ladies of Elizabeth's Court. The alteration in the face of social life, brought about by the recognition of the feminine claim and hastened no doubt by the fact that England, Scotland, and France were at this period under the rule of three ladies of strong character, was inevitably attended with great changes in literature. This change is first expressed by Lyly in his second novel and later in his dramas. The mediaeval conception of women, a masculine conception, now underwent feminine correction ; and what is perhaps of more importance still, the conception of man undergoes transformation also. The result is that the centre of gravity of the story is now shifted. Of old it had treated of deeds and glorious prowess for the sake of honour, or more often for the sake of some anaemic damsel ; now it deals with the passion itself and not its knightly manifestations,—with the very feelings and hearts of the lovers. In other words under the auspices of Elizabeth and her maids of honour, the English story becomes subjective, feminine, its scene is shifted from the battle-field and the lists to the lady's boudoir ; it becomes a novel. "We change lance and war-horse, for walking-sword and pumps and silk stockings. We forget the filletted brows and wind-blown hair, the zone, the flowing robe, the sandalled or buskined feet, and feel the dawning empire of the fan, the glove, the high-heeled shoe, the bonnet, the petticoat, and the parasol[1]": in fact we enter into the modern world. At the first expression of this change in literature *Euphues and his England* is of the very greatest interest. Characters in fiction now for the first time move before a background of everyday life and discuss matters of everyday importance. And, as if Lyly wished to leave no doubt as to his aims and methods, he gives at the conclusion of his book that interesting description of Elizabethan England entitled *A glasse for Europe.*

It is however in Lyly's treatment of the subject of love that the change is most conspicuous. The subtleties of passion are now realised for the first time. We are shown the private emotions, the secret alternations of

---

[1] Bond, I. p. 161.

hope and despair which agitate the breasts of man and maid, and, more important still, we find these emotions at work under the restraint of social conditions; the violent torrent of passion checked and confined by the demands of etiquette and the conventions of aristocratic life. The relation between these unwritten laws of our social constitution and the impetuous ardour of the lover, has formed the main theme of our modern love stories in the novel and on the stage. In the days of chivalry, when love ran wild in the woods, woman was the passive object either of hunt or of rescue; but the scene of battle being shifted to the boudoir she can demand her own conditions with the result that the game becomes infinitely more refined and intricate. Persons of both sexes, outwardly at peace but inwardly armed to the teeth, meet together in some lady's house to discuss the subject so dangerous to both, and conversation conditioned by this fact inevitably becomes subtle, allusive, intense; for it derives its light and shade from the flicker of that fire which the company finds such a perilous fascination in playing with. Lyly's work does not exhibit quite such modernity as this, but we may truthfully say that his *Euphues and his England* is the psychological novel in germ.

Its latent possibilities were however not perceived by the writers of the 16th century. The style which had in part won popularity for it so speedily was the cause also of its equally speedy decline. Like a fossil in the stratum of euphuism it was soon covered up by the artificial layer of arcadianism. The novel of Sidney, though its loose and meandering style marked a reaction against euphuism, carried on the Lylian tradition in its appeal to ladies. The *Arcadia*, in no way so modern as the *Euphues*, lies for that very reason more directly in the line of develop-

ment[1]; for, while the former is linked by the heroical
romance of the seventeenth century to the romance
of this day, the latter's influence is not visible until
the eighteenth century, if we except its immediate
Elizabethan imitators. And yet, as we remarked of
Lyly's prose, a book which received so many editions
cannot have been entirely without effect upon the minds
of its readers and upon the literature of the age. This
influence, however, could have been little more than
suggestive and indirect, and it is quite impossible to
determine its value. Its importance for us lies in the
fact that we can realise how it anticipated the novel of
the 18th and 19th centuries. Not until the days of
Richardson is it possible to detect a Lylian flavour in
English fiction; and even here it would be risky to
insist too pointedly on any inference that might be
drawn from the coincidence of an abridged form of
Euphues being republished (after almost a century's
oblivion) twenty years before the appearance of *Pamela*.
A direct literary connexion between Lyly and Richardson seems out of the question: and the utmost we can
say with certainty is that the novel of the latter, in pro-
viding moral food for its own generation, relieved the
18th century reader of the necessity of going back to
the Elizabethan writer for the entertainment he desired.
As a novelist, therefore, Lyly was only of secondary
dynamical importance, by which I mean that, although
we can rest assured that he exercised a considerable
influence upon later writers, we cannot actually trace
this influence at work; we cannot in fact point to Lyly
as the first of a *definite* series. The novel like its style
coloured, but did not deflect, the stream of English
literature. And indeed we may say this not only of

[1] It was Sidney and Nash who set the fashion for the 17th century.

Euphues but of Elizabethan fiction as a whole. The public to which a 16th century novel would appeal was a small one. Few people in those days could read, and of these the majority preferred to read poetry; and though, as we have seen, *Euphues* passed through, for the age, a considerable number of editions, the circle of those who appreciated Lyly, Sidney, and Nash must have been for the most part confined to the Court. And this accounts for the brevity of their popularity and for its intensity while it lasted; a phenomenon which is not seen in the drama, and which is due to the susceptibility of Court life to sudden changes of fashion. Drama was the natural form of literature in an age when most people were illiterate and yet when all were eager for literary entertainment. Drama was therefore the main current of artistic production, the prose novel being quite a minor, almost an insignificant, tributary. Realising then the inevitable limitations which surrounded our English fiction at its birth we can understand its infantile imperfections and the subsequent arrest of its development.

"The novel held in Elizabeth's time very much the same place as was held by the drama at the Restoration; it was an essentially aristocratic entertainment, and the same pitfall waylaid both, the pitfall of artificiality. Dryden's audiences and the readers of *Euphues* both sought for better bread than is made of wheat; both were supplied with what satisfied them in an elaborate confection of husks[1]."

[1] Raleigh, p. 57. He writes *Arcadia* for *Euphues* but the substitution is legitimate.

CHAPTER III.

LYLY THE DRAMATIST.

So far we have been dealing with those of Lyly's writings, which, though they are his most famous, form quite a small section of his work, and exerted an influence upon later writers which may have been considerable but was certainly indirect. His plays on the other hand, in the production of which he spent the better part of his life, greatly outweigh his novel both in aesthetic and historical importance. To attempt to estimate Lyly's position as a novelist and as a prose writer is to chase the will-o'-the-wisp of theory over the morass of uncertainty; the task of investigating his comedies is altogether simpler and more straightforward. After groping our way through the undergrowth of minor literature, we come out upon the great highway of Elizabethan art—the drama. Let us first see how Lyly himself came to tread this same pathway.

There is a difference of opinion between Mr Bond and Mr Baker, our chief authorities, as to the order in which Lyly wrote his plays[1]. But though Mr Baker claims priority for *Endymion*, and Mr Bond for *Campaspe*,

---

[1] Baker, p. lxxxviii, places *Endymion* as early as Sept. 1579. Bond, vol. III. p. 10, attempts to disprove Baker's contention, and in vol. II. p. 309, he maintains chiefly on grounds of style that *Campaspe* was the earliest of Lyly's plays, being produced at the Christmas of 1580.

both are convinced that our author was already in 1580 beginning to look to the stage as a larger arena for his artistic genius than the novel. And from what I have said of his life at Oxford and his connexion with de Vere, we need not be surprised that this was so. It would be well however at this juncture to recapitulate, and in part to expand those remarks, in order to show more clearly how Lyly's dramatic bent was formed. Seats of learning, as we shall see presently, had long before the days of Lyly favoured the comic muse, and Oxford was no exception to this rule. Anthony à Wood tells us how Richard Edwardes in 1566 produced at that University his play *Palamon and Arcite*, and how her Majesty "laughed heartily thereat and gave the author great thanks for his pains"; a scene which would still be fresh in men's minds five years after, when Lyly entered Magdalen College. But it is scarcely necessary to stretch a point here since we know from the *Anatomy of Wit* that Lyly was a student of Edwardes' comedies[1]. Again, William Gager, Pettie's "dear friend" and Lyly's fellow-student, was a dramatist, while Gosson himself tells us of comedies which he had written before 1577.

Probably however it was not until he had left Oxford for London that Lyly conceived the idea of writing comedy, for we must attribute its original suggestion to his friend and employer the Earl of Oxford. Edward de Vere, Burleigh's son-in-law, had visited Italy, and affected the vices and artificialities of that country, returning home, we are told, laden with silks and oriental stuffs for the adornment of his chamber and his person. He was frequently in debt and still more frequently in disgrace with the Queen and with his father-in-law. Dilettante, aesthete, and euphuist, he would naturally

[1] Bond, II. p. 238.

attract the Oxford fop, and that Lyly attached himself to his clique disposes, in my mind at least, of all theories of his puritanical tendencies. Certainly a Nonconformist conscience could not have flourished in de Vere's household. One bond between the Earl and his secretary was their love of music—an art which played an important part in the beginning of our comedy.

In relieving the action of his plays by those songs of woodland beauty unmatched in literature Shakespeare was only following a custom set by his predecessors, Udall, Edwardes, and Lyly, who being schoolmasters (and the two latter being musicians and holding positions in choir schools), embroidered their comedies with lyrics to be sung by the fresh young voices of their pupils. De Vere, though unconnected with a school, probably followed the same tradition. For the interesting thing about him is that he also wrote comedy. Like many members of the nobility in those days he maintained his own company of players; and we find them in 1581 giving performances at Cambridge and Ipswich. His comedies, moreover, though now lost were placed in the same rank as those of Edwardes by the Elizabethan critic Puttenham[1]. Now as secretary of such a man, and therefore in close intimacy with him, it would be the most natural thing in the world for Lyly to try his hand at play-writing, and, if his patron approved of his efforts, an introduction to Court could be procured, since Oxford was Lord High Chamberlain, and the play would be acted. It was to Oxford's patronage, therefore, and not to his subsequent connexion with the "children of Powles," that Lyly owed his first dramatic impulse, and probably also his first dramatic success, for *Campaspe* and *Sapho* were produced at Court in 1582[2]. His

[1] *Dict. of Nat. Biog.*, Edward de Vere.
[2] Bond, II. p. 230 (chronological table).

appointment at the choir school of course confirmed his
resolutions and thus he became the first great Elizabethan
dramatist.

But a purely circumstantial explanation of an important departure in a man's life will only appear satisfactory
to fatalists who worship the blind god Environment.
And without indulging in any abstruse psychological
discussion, but rather looking at the question from
a general point of view, we can understand how an
intellect of Lyly's type, as revealed by the *Euphues*,
found its ultimate expression in comedy.   Comedy, as
Meredith tells us, is only possible in a civilized society,
"where ideas are current and the perceptions quick."
We have already touched upon this point and later we
must return to it again ; but for the moment let us
notice that this idea of comedy, though he would have
been quite unable to formulate it in words, was in reality
at the back of Lyly's mind, or rather we should perhaps
say that he quite unconsciously embodied it.   He was
par excellence the product of a "social" atmosphere ; he
moved more freely within the Court than without ; his
whole mind was absorbed by the subtleties of language ;
a brilliant conversation, an apt repartee, a well-turned
phrase were the very breath of his nostrils ; his ideal
was the intellectual beau.   Add to this compound the
ingredient of literary ambition and the result is a comic
dramatist.   Lyly, Congreve, Sheridan, were all men
of fashion first and writers of comedy after.   In the
author of *Lady Windermere's Fan* we have lately seen
another example—the example of one whose ambition
was to be "the first well-dressed philosopher in the
history of thought."   Poems, novels, fairy stories, he
gave us, but it was on the stage of comedy that he
eventually found his true *métier*.   "With *Euphues*,"
writes Mr Bond, "we enter the path which leads to the

Restoration dramatists......and in Lucilla and Camilla we are prescient of Millamant and Belinda[1]." This is very true, but the statement has a nearer application which Mr Bond misses. Camilla is the lady who moves under varied names through all Lyly's plays. The second part of *Euphues* and the first of Lyly's comedies are as closely connected psychologically and aesthetically, as they were in point of time.

SECTION I. *English Comedy before* 1580.

But when Lyly's creations began to walk the boards, the English stage was already some centuries old and therefore, in order to appreciate our author's position, a few words are necessary upon the development of our drama and especially of comedy previous to his time.

Though the *miracle* play of our forefathers frequently contained a species of coarse humour usually put into the mouth of the Devil, who appears to have been for the middle ages very much what the "comic muse" is for us moderns, it is to the *morality* not to the *miracle* that one should look for the real beginnings of comedy as distinct from mere buffoonery.

The *morality* was not so much an offshoot as a complement of the *miracle*. They stood to each other, as sermon does to service. To say therefore that the *morality* secularized the drama is to go too far; as well might we say that Luther secularized Christianity. What it did, however, was important enough; it severed the connexion between drama and ritual. The *miracle*, treating of the history of mankind from the Creation to the days of Christ, unfolded before the eyes of its

[1] Bond, I. p. 161.

audience the grand scheme of human salvation ; the *morality* on the other hand was not concerned with historical so much as practical Christianity. Its object was to point a moral : and it did this in two ways ; either as an affirmative, constructive inculcator of what life should be,—as the portrayer of the ideal ; or as a negative, critical describer of the types of life actually existing,—as the portrayer of the real. It approached more nearly to comedy in its latter function, but in both aspects it really prepared the way for the comic muse. The natural prey of comedy, as our greatest comic writer has taught us, is folly, "known to it in all her transformations, in every disguise ; and it is with the springing delight of hawk over heron, hound after fox, that it gives her chase, never fretting, never tiring, sure of having her, allowing her no rest." Thus it is that characters in comedy, symbolizing as they often do some social folly, tend to be rather types than personalities. The *morality*, therefore, in substituting typical figures, however crude, for the mechanical religious characters of the *miracle*, makes an immense advance towards comedy. Moreover, the very selection of types requires an appreciation, if not an analysis, of the differences of human character, an appreciation for which there was no need in the *miracle*. In the *morality* again the action is no longer determined by tradition, and it becomes incumbent on the playwright to provide motives for the movements of his puppets. It follows naturally from this that situations must be devised to show up the particular quality which each type symbolizes. We need not enter the vexed question of the origin of plot construction ; but we may notice in this connexion that the *morality* certainly gave us that peculiar form of plot-movement which is most suitable to comedy. To quote

Mr Gayley's words: "In tragedy, the movement must be economic of its ups and downs; once headed downwards it must plunge, with but one or two vain recovers, to the abyss. In comedy, on the other hand, though the movement is ultimately upward, the crises are more numerous; the oftener the individual stumbles without breaking his neck, and the more varied his discomfitures, so long as they are temporary, the better does he enjoy his ease in the cool of the day..........Now the novelty of the plot in the *moral* play, lay in the fact that the movement was of this oscillating, upward kind—a kind unknown as a rule to the *miracle*, whose conditions were less fluid, and to the farce, which was too shallow and superficial[1]."

If all these claims be justifiable there can be no doubt that the *morality* was of the utmost importance in the history not only of comedy but of English drama as a whole. Though it was the cousin, not the child of the *miracle*, though it cannot be said to have secularized our drama, it is the link between the ritual play and the play of pure amusement; it connects the rood gallery with the London theatre. When Symonds writes that the *morality* "can hardly be said to lie in the direct line of evolution between the *miracle* and the legitimate drama" we may in part agree with him; but he is quite wrong when he goes on to describe it as "an abortive side-effect, which was destined to bear barren fruit[2]."

The real secularization of the drama was in the first place probably due to classical influences—or, to be more precise, I should perhaps say, scholastic influences —and it is not until the 16th century that these influences become prominent. I say "become prominent,"

---

[1] Gayley, p. lxiv.   [2] Symonds, p. 199.

because Terence and Plautus were known from the earliest times, and Dr Ward is inclined to think that Latin comedy affected the earlier drama of England to a considerable extent[1], although good examples of Terentian comedy are not found until the 16th century. Humanism again comes forward as an important literary formative element. The part which the student class took in the development of European drama as a whole has as yet scarcely been appreciated. It is to scholars that the birth of the secular Drama must be attributed. Lyly, as we said, made use of his mastership for the production of his plays, but Lyly was by no means the first schoolmaster-dramatist. Schools and universities had long before his day been productive of drama; our very earliest existing saints' play or *marvel* was produced by a certain Geoffrey at Dunstable, "de consuetudine magistrorum et scholarum[2]." And this was only natural, seeing that at such places any number of actors is available and all are supposed to be interested in literature. It is a remarkable fact, however, and illustrative of the connexion between comedy and music, that of all places of education choir schools seem to have usurped the lion's share of drama. John Heywood, the first to break away from the tradition of the *morality*, was a choir boy of the Chapel Royal, and afterwards in all probability held a post there as master[3]. Heywood's brilliant, but farcical interludes are too slight to merit the title of comedy, yet he is of great importance because of his rejection of allegories and of his use of "personal types" instead of "personified

[1] Ward, I. p. 7.

[2] Gayley, p. xiv.

[3] I put this interpretation upon the account of Heywood's receiving 40 shillings from Queen Mary "for pleying an interlude with his children."

abstractions[1]." It was not until 1540, a few years after
Heywood's interlude *The Play of the Wether*, that pure
English comedy appears, and we must turn to Eton to
discover its cradle, for Nicholas Udall's *Roister Doister*
has every claim to rank as the first completely constructed comedy in our language—the first comedy of
flesh and blood. Roister smacks of the "miles gloriosus";
Merygreeke combines the vice with the Terentian rogue;
and yet, when all is said, Udall's play remains a remark-
ably original production, realistic and English.

Next, in point of time and importance, comes
Stevenson's *Gammer Gurton's Needle*, still more
thoroughly English than the last, though quite inferior
as a comedy, and indeed scarcely rising above the level
of farce. Inasmuch, however, as it is a drama of English
rustic life, it is directly antecedent to *Mother Bombie*,
and perhaps also to the picaresque novel. Secular
dramas now began to multiply apace. But keeping our
eye upon comedy, and upon Lyly in particular as we
near the date of his advent, it will be sufficient I think
to mention two more names to complete the chain of
development. From Cambridge, the nurse of Stevenson,
we must now turn to Oxford; and, as we do so, we seem
to be drawing very close to the end of our journey.
Thus far we have had nothing like the romantic comedy
—the comedy of sentiment, of love, the comedy which
is at once serious and witty, and which contains the
elements of tragedy. This appears, or is at least fore-
shadowed for the first time, about four years after
Stevenson's "first-rate screaming farce," as Symonds
has dubbed it, in the *Damon and Pithias* of Richard
Edwardes, a writer with whom, as we have seen, Lyly
was thoroughly familiar. Indeed, the play in question

---

[1] Ward, *Dict. of Nat. Biog.*, Heywood.

anticipates our author in many ways, for example in the introduction of pages, in the use of English proverbs and Latin quotations, and in the insertion of songs[1]. With reference to the last point, we may remark that Edwardes like Lyly was interested in music, and like him also held a post in a choir school, being one of the "gentlemen of the Chapel Royal." In the *Damon and Pithias* the old *morality* is once and for all discarded. The play is entirely free from all allegorical elements, and is only faintly tinged with didacticism. But we cannot express the aim of Edwardes better than in his own words:

> "In comedies the greatest skyll is this, lightly to touch
> All thynges to the quick; and eke to frame each person so
> That by his common talke, you may his nature rightly know."

To touch lightly and yet with penetration, to reveal character by dialogue, this is indeed to write modern drama, modern comedy.

It would seem that between Edwardes and Lyly there was no room for another link, so closely does the one follow the other; and yet one more play must be mentioned to complete the series. This time we are no longer brought into touch with the classics or with the scholastic influences, for the play in question is a translation from the Italian, being in fact Ariosto's *Suppositi*, englished by George Gascoigne[2]. Though a translation it was more than a transcript; it was englished in the true sense of that word, in sentiment as well as in phrase. Its chief importance lies in the fact that it is written in prose, and is therefore the first prose comedy in our language. But Mr Gayley would go further than this, for he describes it as "the first English comedy in every way worthy of the name."

---

[1] Bond, II. p. 238.   [2] 1566.

It was written entirely for amusement, and for the amusement of adults, not of children ; and if it were the only product of Gascoigne's pen it would justify the remark of an early 17th century critic, who says of this writer that he "brake the ice for our quainter poets who now write, that they may more safely swim through the main ocean of sweet poesy"; for, to quote a modern writer, "with the blood of the New comedy, the Latin comedy, the Renaissance in its veins, it is far ahead of its English contemporaries, if not of its time[1]." The play was well known and popular among the Elizabethans, being revived at Oxford in 1582[2]. Shakespeare used it for the construction of his *Taming of the Shrew*: and altogether it is difficult to say how much Elizabethan drama probably owed to this one comedy, which though Italian in origin was carefully adapted to English taste by its translator. There can be no doubt that Lyly studied this among other of Gascoigne's works, and that he must have learnt many lessons from it, though the fact does not appear to have been sufficiently appreciated by Lylian students; for even Mr Bond fails, I think, to realise its importance.

This, in brief outline, is the history of our comedy down to the time when Lyly took it in hand ; or should we not rather say "an introduction to the history of our comedy"? For true English comedy is not to be found in any of the plays we have mentioned. Heywood, Udall, Stevenson, Edwardes, are the names that convey "broken lights" of comedy, hints of the dawn, nothing more ; and Gascoigne was a translator. The supreme importance of a writer, who at this juncture produced eight comedies of sustained merit, and of varying types, is something which is quite beyond computation. But

---

[1] Gayley, p. lxxxv.   [2] *Dict. of Nat. Biog.*, Gascoigne, George.

if we are to attempt to realise the greatness of our debt
to Lyly, let us estimate exactly how much these previous
efforts had done in the way of pioneer work, and how far
also they fell short of comedy in the strict sense of that
word.

The fifty years which lie between Heywood and Lyly
saw considerable progress, but progress of a negative
rather than a constructive nature, and moreover progress
which came in fits and starts, and not continuously. It
was in fact a period of transition and of individual and
disconnected experiments. Each of the writers above
mentioned contributed something towards the common
development, but not one of them, except Ariosto's
translator, gave us comedy which may be considered
complete in every way. They all display a very
elementary knowledge of plot construction. Udall is
perhaps the most successful in this respect ; his plot is
trivial but, well versed as he is in Terence, he manages
to give it an ordered and natural development. But the
other pre-Lylian dramatists quite failed to realise the
vital importance of plot, which is indeed the very essence
of comedy; and, in expending energies upon the development of an argument, as in *Jacke Jugeler*, which was a
parody of transubstantiation, or upon the construction
of disconnected humorous situations, as in *Gammer
Gurton's Needle*, they missed the whole point of comedy.
Again, though there is a clear idea of distinction and
interplay of characters, there is little perception of the
necessity of developing character as the plot moves
forward. Merygreeke, it may be objected, is an example
of such development, but the alteration in Merygreeke's
nature is due to inconsistency, not to evolution. Moreover, stage conventions had not yet become a matter of
fixed tradition. "We have a perpetual conflict between

what spectators actually see and what they are supposed
to see, between the time actually passed and that sup-
posed to have elapsed ; an outrageous demand on the
imagination in one place, a refusal to exercise or allow
us to exercise it in another[1]." Further, English comedy
before 1580 was marked, on the one hand, by its poetic
literary form and, on the other, by its almost complete
absence of poetic ideas. Lyly, with the instinct of a
born conversationalist, realised that prose was the only
possible dress for comedy that should seek to represent
contemporary life. But even in their use of verse his
predecessors were unsuccessful. Udall seemed to have
thought that his unequal dogtail lines would wag if he
struck a rhyme at the end, and even Edwardes was little
better. The use of blank verse had yet to be discovered,
and Lyly was to have a hand in this matter also[2]. As
for poetical treatment of comedy, Edwardes is the only
one who even approaches it. He does so, because he
sees that the comic muse only ceases to be a mask when
sentiment is allowed to play over her features. And
even he only half perceives it ; for the sentiment of
friendship is not strong enough for complete animation,
the muse's eyes may twinkle, but passion alone will give
them depth and let the soul shine through. But, in
order that passion should fill comedy with the breath
of life, it was necessary that both sexes should walk the
stage on an equal footing. That which comedy before
1580 lacked, that which alone could round it off into a
poetic whole, was the female element. "Comedy," writes
George Meredith, "lifts women to a station offering
them free play for their wit, as they usually show it,

---

[1] Bond, II. p. 237.

[2] George Gascoigne, whose importance does not seem to have been
realised by Elizabethan students, also produced a drama in blank verse.

when they have it, on the side of sound sense. The higher the comedy, the more prominent the part they enjoy in it." But the dramatist cannot lift them far; the civilized plane must lie only just beneath the comic plane; the stage cannot be lighted by woman's wit if the audience have not yet realised that brain forms a part of the feminine organism. In the days of Elizabeth this realisation began to dawn in men's minds; but it was Lyly who first expressed it in literature, in his novel and then in his dramas. Those who preceded him were only dimly conscious of it, and therefore they failed to seize upon it as material for art. It was at Court, the Court of a great virgin Queen, that the equality of social privileges for women was first established; it was a courtier who introduced heroines into our drama.

Section II. *The Eight Plays.*

Concerning the order of Lyly's plays there is, as we have seen, some difference of opinion. The discussion between Mr Bond and Mr Baker in reality turns upon the interpretation of the allegory of *Endymion*, and it is therefore one of those questions of literary probability which can never hope to receive a satisfactory answer. Both critics, however, are in agreement as to the proper method of classification. They divide the dramas into four categories: historical, of which *Campaspe* is the sole example; allegorical, which includes *Sapho and Phao*, *Endymion*, and *Midas*; pastoral, which includes *Gallathea*, *The Woman in the Moon*, and *Love's Metamorphosis*; and lastly realistic, of which again there is only one example, *Mother Bombie*. The fault which may be found with this classification is that the so-called pastoral plays have much of the allegorical about them, and it is perhaps better, therefore, to consider them rather as a subdivision of class two than as a distinct species.

For the moment putting on one side all questions of the allegory of *Endymion*, there are two reasons which seem to go a long way towards justifying Mr Bond for placing *Campaspe* as the earliest of Lyly's plays. In the first place the atmosphere of *Euphues*, which becomes weaker in the other plays, is so unmistakeable in this historical drama as to force the conclusion upon us that they belong to the same period. The painter Apelles, whose name seemed almost to obsess Lyly in his novel, is one of the chief characters of *Campaspe,* and the dialogue is more decidedly euphuistic than any other play. The second point we may notice is one which can leave very little doubt as to the correctness of Mr Bond's chronology. *Campaspe* and *Sapho* were published before 1585, that is, before Lyly accepted the mastership at the St Paul's choir school, whereas none of his other plays came into the printer's hands until after the inhibition of the boys' acting rights in 1591; the obvious inference being that Lyly printed his plays only when he had no interest in preserving the acting rights.

But whatever date we assign to *Campaspe*, there can be little doubt that it was one of the first dramas in our language with an historical background. Indeed, *Kynge Johan* is the only play before 1580 which can claim to rival it in this respect. But *Kynge Johan* was written solely for the purpose of religious satire, being an attack upon the priesthood and Church abuses. It must, there-fore, be classed among those political *moralities*, of which so many examples appeared during the early part of the 16th century. *Campaspe*, on the other hand, is entirely devoid of any ethical or satirical motive. Allegory,

7—2

which Lyly was able to put to his own peculiar uses,
is here quite absent. The sole aim of its author was to
provide amusement, and in this respect it must have
been entirely successful. The play is interesting, and at
times amusing, even to a modern reader; but to those
who witnessed its performance at Blackfriars, and, two
years later, at the Court, it would appear as a marvel of
wit and dramatic power after the crude material which
had hitherto been offered to them. In the choice of his
subject Lyly shows at once that he is an artist with a
feeling for beauty, even if he seldom rises to its sublimi-
ties. The story of the play, taken from Pliny, is that of
Alexander's love for his Theban captive Campaspe, and
of his subsequent self-sacrifice in giving her up to her
lover Apelles. The social change, which I have sought
to indicate in the preceding pages, is at once evident in
this play. "We calling Alexander from his grave," says
its Prologue[1], "seeke only who was his love"; and the
remark is a sweep of the hat to the ladies of the Court,
whose importance, as an integral part of the audience, is
now for the first time openly acknowledged. "Alexander,
the great conqueror of the world," says Lyly with his
hand upon his heart, "only interests me as a lover."
The whole motive of the play, which would have been
meaningless to a mediaeval audience, is a compliment to
the ladies. It is as if our author nets Mars with Venus,
and presents the shamefaced god as an offering of flattery
to the Queen and her Court. *Campaspe* is, in fact, the
first romantic drama, not only the forerunner of Shakespeare, but a remote ancestor of *Hernani* and the 19th
century French theatre. "The play's defect," says
Mr Bond, "is one of passion"—a criticism which is
applicable to all Lyly's dramas; and yet we must not

---

[1] From *Prologue* at the Court.

forget that Lyly was the earliest to deal with passion dramatically. The love of Alexander is certainly un-emotional, not to say callous; but possibly the great monarch's equanimity was a veiled tribute to the sup-posed indifference of the virgin Queen to all matters of Cupid's trade. Between Campaspe and Apelles, how-ever, we have scenes which are imbued, if not vitalized, by passion. Lyly was a beginner, and his fault lay in attempting too much. Caring more for brilliancy of dialogue than for anything else, he was no more likely to be successful here, in portraying passion through con-versation weighted by euphuism, than he had been in his novel. Yet his endeavour to depict the conflict of mas-culine passion with feminine wit, impatient sallies neatly parried, deliberate lunges quietly turned aside, was in every way praiseworthy. "A witte apt to conceive and quickest to answer" is attributed by Alexander to Cam-paspe, and, though she exhibits few signs of it, yet in his very idea of endowing women with wit Lyly leads us on to the high-road of comedy leading to Congreve.

In addition to the romantic elements above described, we have here also that page-prattle which is so charac-teristic of all Lyly's plays. These urchins, full of mischief and delighting in quips, were probably borrowed from Edwardes, but Lyly made them all his own; and one can understand how naturally their parts would be played by his boy-actors. Their repartee, when it is not pulling to pieces some Latin quotation familiar to them at school, or ridiculing a point of logic, is often really witty. One of them, overhearing the hungry Manes at strife with Diogenes over the matter of an overdue dinner, exclaims to his friend, "This is their use, nowe do they dine one upon another." Diogenes again, in whom we may see the prototype of Shakespeare's Timon, is amusing enough at times with his "dogged" snarlings and sallies which frequently however miss their mark.   He and the pages form an underplot of farce, upon which Lyly improved in his later plays, bringing it also more into connexion with the main plot.   In passing, we may notice that few of Shakespeare's plays are without this farcical substratum.

Leaving the question of dramatic construction and characterization for a more general treatment later, we now pass on to the consideration of Lyly's allegorical plays.   The absence of all allegory from *Campaspe* shows that Lyly had broken with the *morality*: and we seem therefore to be going back, when two years later we have an allegorical play from his pen.   But in reality there is no retrogression; for with Lyly allegory is not an ethical instrument.   I have mentioned examples of plays before his day which employed the machinery of the *morality*, for the purposes of political and religious satire.   The old form of drama seems to have developed a keen sensibility to *double entendre* among theatre-goers. Nothing indeed is so remarkable about the Elizabethan stage as the secret understanding which almost invariably existed between the dramatist and his audience. We have already had occasion to notice it in connexion with Field's parody of Kyd.   The spectators were always on the alert to detect some veiled reference to prominent political figures or to current affairs.   Often in fact, as was natural, they would discover hints where nothing was implied; and for one Mrs Gallup in modern America there must have been a dozen in every auditorium of Elizabethan England.   Such over-clever busybodies would readily twist an innocent remark into treason or sacrilege, and therefore, long before Lyly's time, it was customary for a playwright to defend himself in the prologue against such treatment, by denying any ambiguity in his dialogue. In an audience thus susceptible to innuendo Lyly saw his opportunity. He was a courtier writing for the Court, he was also, let us add, anxious to obtain a certain coveted post at the Revels' Office. He was an artist not entirely without ideals, yet ever ready to curry favour and to aim at material advantages by his literary facility. The idea therefore of writing dramas which should be, from beginning to end, nothing but an ingenious compliment to his royal mistress would not be in the least distasteful to him. But we must not attribute too much to motives of personal ambition. Spenser's *Faery Queen* was not published until 1590; but Lyly had known Spenser before the latter's departure for Ireland, and, even if the scheme of that poet's masterpiece had not been confided to him, the ideas which it contained were in the air. The cult of Elizabeth, which was far from being a piece of insincere adulation, had for some time past been growing into a kind of literary religion. Even to us, there is something magical about the great Queen, and we can hardly be surprised that the pagans of those days hailed her as half divine. When Lyly commenced his career, she had been on the throne for twenty years, in itself a wonderful fact to those who could remember the gloom which had surrounded her accession. Through a period of infinite danger both at home and abroad she had guided England with intrepidity and success; and furthermore she had done all this single-handed, refusing to share her throne with a partner even for the sake of protection, and yet improving upon the Habsburg policy[1] by making coquetry the pivot of her diplomacy. It was no wonder therefore that,

[1] " Alii bella gerunt, tu felix Austria nube."

> "As the imperial votaress passed on
> In maiden meditation fancy free,"

the courtiers she fondled, and the artists she patronized,
should half in fancy, half in earnest, think of her as
something more than human, and search the fables of
their newly discovered classics for examples of enthroned
chastity and unconquerable virgin queens.

All Lyly's plays except *Campaspe* and *Mother Bombie*
are written in this vein; each, as Symonds beautifully
puts it, is "a censer of exquisitely chased silver, full of
incense to be tossed before Elizabeth upon her throne."
In the three plays *Sapho and Phao*, *Endymion*, and
Midas this element of flattery is more prominent than
in the others, inasmuch as they are not only full of compliments unmistakeably directed towards the Queen, but
they actually seek to depict incidents from her reign
under the guise of classical mythology. It is for this
reason that they have been classified under the label of
allegory. It is quite possible, however, to read and enjoy
these plays without a suspicion of any inner meaning;
nor does the absence of such suspicion render the action
of the play in any way unintelligible, so skilfully does
Lyly manipulate his story. With a view, therefore, to
his position in the history of Elizabethan drama, and to
the lessons which he taught those who came after him,
the superficial interpretation of each play is all that need
engage our attention, and we shall content ourselves
with briefly indicating the actual incident which it
symbolizes.

The story of *Sapho and Phao* is, very shortly, as
follows. Phao, a poor ferryman, is endowed by Venus
with the gift of beauty. Sapho, who in Lyly's hands
is stripped of all poetical attributes and becomes simply
a great Queen of Sicily, sees him and instantly falls in

love with him. To conceal her passion, she pretends to her ladies that she has a fever, at the same time sending for Phao, who is rumoured to have herbs for such complaints. Meanwhile Venus herself falls a victim to the charms she has bestowed upon the ferryman. Cupid is therefore called in to remedy matters on her behalf. The boy, who plays a part which no one can fail to compare with that of Puck in the *Midsummer Night's Dream*, succeeds in curing Sapho's passion, but, much to his mother's disgust, won over by the Queen's attractions, refuses to go further, and even inspires Phao with a loathing for the goddess. The play ends with Phao's departure from Sicily in despair, and Cupid's definite rebellion from the rule of Venus, resulting in his remaining with Sapho. In this story, which is practically a creation of Lyly's brain, though of course it is founded upon the classical tale of Sapho's love for Phao, our playwright presents under the form of allegory the history of Alençon's courtship of Elizabeth. Sapho, Queen of Sicily, is of course Elizabeth, Queen of England. The difficulty of Alençon's (that is Phao's) ugliness is overcome by the device of making it love's task to confer beauty upon him. Phao like Alençon quits the island and its Queen in despair; while the play is rounded off by the pretty compliment of representing love as a willing captive in Elizabeth's Court.

As a play *Sapho and Phao* shows a distinct advance upon *Campaspe*. The dialogue is less euphuistic, and therefore much more effective. The conversation between Sapho and Phao, in the scene where the latter comes with his herbs to cure the Queen, is very charming, and well expresses the passion which the one is too humble and the other too proud to show.

PHAO. I know no hearb to make lovers sleepe but Heartesease, which because it groweth so high, I cannot reach : for—

SAPHO. For whom?

PHAO. For such as love.

SAPHO. It groweth very low, and I can never stoop to it, that—

PHAO. That what?

SAPHO. That I may gather it : but why doe you sigh so, Phao?

PHAO. It is mine use Madame.

SAPHO. It will doe you harme and mee too : for I never heare one sighe, but I must sigh't also.

PHAO. It were best then that your Ladyship give me leave to be gone : for I can but sigh.

SAPHO. Nay stay : for now I beginne to sighe, I shall not leave though you be gone. But what do you thinke best for your sighing to take it away?

PHAO. Yew, Madame.

SAPHO. Mee?

PHAO. No Madame, yewe of the tree.

SAPHO. Then will I love yewe the better, and indeed I think it should make me sleepe too, therefore all other simples set aside, I will simply use onely yewe.

PHAO. Doe Madame : for I think nothing in the world so good as yewe[1].

Altogether there is a great increase in general vitality in this play. Lyly draws nearer to the conception of ideal comedy. "Our interest," he tells us in his Prologue, "was at this time to move inward delight not

[1] *Sapho and Phao*, Act III. Sc. IV. 60–85.

outward lightnesse, and to breede (if it might be) soft smiling, not loud laughing"; and to this end he tends to minimize the purely farcical element. The pages are still present, but they are balanced by a group of Sapho's maids-in-waiting who discuss the subject of love upon the stage with great frankness and charm. Mileta, the leader of this chorus, is, we may suspect, a portrait drawn from life; she is certainly much more convincing than the somewhat shadowy Campaspe. The figures in Lyly's studio are limited in number—Camilla, Lucilla, Campaspe, Mileta, all come from the same mould: in Pandion we may discover Euphues under a new name, and the surly Vulcan is only another edition of the "crabbed Diogenes." And yet each of these types becomes more life-like as he proceeds, and if the puppets that he left to his successors were not yet human, they had learnt to walk the stage without that angularity of movement and jerkiness of speech which betray the machine.

Departing for a moment from the strictly chrono- logical order, and leaving *Gallathea* for later treatment, we pass on to *Endymion*, the second of the allegorical dramas, and, without doubt, the boldest in conception and the most beautiful in execution of all Lyly's plays. The story is founded upon the classical fable of Diana's kiss to the sleeping boy, but its arrangement and de- velopment are for the most part of Lyly's invention: indeed, he was obliged to frame it in accordance with the facts which he sought to allegorize. All critics are agreed in identifying Cynthia with Elizabeth and En- dymion with Leicester, but they part company upon the interpretation of the play as a whole. The story is briefly as follows. Endymion, forsaking his former love Tellus, contracts an ardent passion for Cynthia, who, in accordance with her character as moon-goddess, meets his advances with coolness. Tellus determines to be revenged, and, by the aid of a sorceress Dipsas, sends the youth into a deep sleep from which no one can awaken him. Cynthia learns what has befallen, and although she does not suspect Tellus, she orders the latter to be shut up in a castle for speaking maliciously of Endymion. She then sends Eumenides, the young man's great friend, to seek out a remedy. This man is deeply in love with Semele, who scorns his passion, and therefore, when he reaches a magic fountain which will answer any question put to it, he is so absorbed with his own troubles as almost to forget those of his friend. A carefully thought-out piece of writing follows, for he debates with himself whether to use his one question for an enquiry about his love or his sleeping friend. Friendship and duty conquer at length, and, looking into the well, he discovers that the remedy for Endymion's sickness is a kiss from Cynthia's lips. He returns with his message, the kiss is given, Endymion, grown old after 40 years' sleep, is restored to youth, the treachery of Tellus is discovered and eventually forgiven, and the play ends amid a peal of marriage bells. Endymion, however, is left unmarried, knowing as he does that lowly and distant worship is all he can be allowed to offer the virgin goddess. The play, of course, has a farcical underplot which is only connected very slightly with the main story by Sir Tophas' ridiculous passion for Dipsas. His love in fact is presented as a kind of caricature of Endymion's, and he is the laughing-stock of a number of pages who gambol and play pranks after the usual manner of Lyly's boys. The solution of the allegory lies mainly in the interpretation of Tellus' character, and I cannot but agree with Mr Bond when he decides that Tellus is Mary Queen of Scots. He is perhaps less convincing where he pairs Endymion with Sidney, and Semele with Penelope Devereux, the famous *Stella*. Lastly we may notice his suggestion that Tophas may be Gabriel Harvey, which certainly appears to be more probable than Halpin's theory that Stephen Gosson is here meant[1]. But the whole question is one of such obscurity, and of so little importance from the point of view of my argument, that I shall not attempt to enter further into it.

In *Endymion* Lyly shows that his mastership of St Paul's has increased his knowledge of stage-craft. For example, while *Campaspe* contains at least four imaginary transfers in space in the middle of a scene, *Endymion* has only one: and it is a transfer which requires a much smaller stretch of imagination than the constant appearance of Diogenes' tub upon the stage whenever and wherever comic relief was considered necessary. There is improvement moreover in characterization. But the interesting thing about this play is Shakespeare's intimate knowledge of it, visible chiefly in the *Midsummer Night's Dream*. The well-known speech of Oberon to Puck, directing him to gather the "little western flower," is to all intents and purposes a beautiful condensation of Lyly's allegory. One would like, indeed, to think that there was something more than fancy in Mr Gollancz's suggestion that Shakespeare when a boy had seen this play of Lyly's acted at Kenilworth, where Leicester entertained Elizabeth ; little William going thither with his father from the neighbouring town of Stratford. But however that may be, *Endymion* certainly had a peculiar fascination for him ; we may even detect borrowings from the

---

[1] Halpin, *Oberon's Vision*, Shakespeare Society, 1843.

underplot. Tophas' enumeration of the charms of
Dipsas[1] foreshadows Thisbe's speech over the fallen
Pyramus[2], while, did we not know Lyly's play to be the
earlier, we might suspect the page's song near the sleeping knight to be a clumsy caricature of the graceful
songs of the fairies guarding Titania's dreams. Again
there are parallels in Shakespeare's earliest comedy
Love's Labour's Lost. Sir Tophas, who is undoubtedly
modelled upon Roister Doister, reappears with his page,
as Armado with his attendant Moth. And I have no
doubt that many other resemblances might be discovered by careful investigation. We cannot wonder
that *Endymion* attracted Shakespeare, for it is the
most "romantic" of all Lyly's plays. Indistinctness of
character seems to be in keeping with an allegory of
moonshine ; and even the mechanical action cannot
spoil the poetical atmosphere which pervades the whole.
Here if anywhere Lyly reached the poetical plane. He
speaks of "thoughts stitched to the starres," of "time
that treadeth all things down but truth," of the "ivy
which, though it climb up by the elme, can never get
hold of the beames of the sunne," and the play is full of
many other quaint poetical conceits.

From the point of view of drama, however, it cannot
be considered equal to the third of the allegorical plays.
As a man of fashion Lyly was nothing if not up to date.
In August 1588 the great Armada had made its abortive
attack upon Cynthia's kingdom, and twelve months were
scarcely gone before the industrious Court dramatist had
written and produced on the stage an allegorical satire
upon his Catholic Majesty Philip, King of Spain. Though
it contains compliments to Elizabeth, *Midas* is more of

---

[1] *Endymion*, Act III. Sc. II. ll. 30–60.
[2] Cp. also Shakespeare, *Sonnet* CXXX.

a patriotic than a purely Court play. The story, with but a few necessary alterations, comes from Ovid's *Metamorphoses*[1]. It is the old tale of the three wishes. Love, power, and wealth are offered, and Midas chooses the last. But he soon finds that the gift of turning everything to gold has its drawbacks. Even his beard accidentally becomes bullion. He eventually gets rid of his obnoxious power by bathing in a river. The fault of the play is that there are, as it were, two sections; for now we are introduced to an entirely new situation. The King chances upon Apollo and Pan engaged in a musical contest, and, asked to decide between them, gives his verdict for the goat-foot god. Apollo, in revenge, endows him with a pair of ass's ears. For some time he manages to conceal them; but "murder will out," for the reeds breathe the secret to the wind. Midas in the end seeks pardon at Apollo's shrine, and is relieved of his ears. At the same time he abandons his project of invading the neighbouring island of Lesbos, to which continual references are made throughout the play. This island is of course England; the golden touch refers to the wealth of Spanish America, while, if Halpin be correct, Pan and Apollo signify the Catholic and the Protestant faith respectively. We may also notice, in passing, that the ears obviously gave Shakespeare the idea of Bottom's "transfiguration."

The weakness of the play, as I have said, lies in its duality of action. In other respects, however, it is certainly a great advance on its predecessors, especially in its underplot, which is for the first time connected satisfactorily with the main argument. Motto, the royal barber, in the course of his duties, obtains possession of the golden beard: and the history of this somewhat

[1] XI. 85–193.

unusual form of treasure affords a certain amount of amusing farcical relief. It is stolen by one of the Court pages, Motto recovers it as a reward for curing the thief's toothache, but he loses it again because, being overheard hinting at the ass's ears, he is convicted of treason by the pages, and is blackmailed in consequence. From this it will be seen that the underplot is more embroidered with incident and is, in every way, better arranged than in the earlier plays.

We must now turn to the pastoral plays, *Gallathea*, *The Woman in the Moon*, and *Love's Metamorphosis*, which we may consider together since their stories, uninspired by any allegorical purpose beyond general compliments to the Queen, do not require any detailed consideration. And yet it should be pointed out that this distinction between Lyly's allegorical and pastoral plays is more apparent than real. There are shepherds in *Midas*, the Queen appears under the mythological title of Ceres in *Love's Metamorphosis*. Such overlapping however is only to be expected, and the division is at least very convenient for purposes of classification. Lyly's pastoral plays form, as it were, a link between the drama and the masque; indeed, when we consider that all the Elizabethan dramatists were students of Lyly, it is possible that comedy and masque may have been evolved from the Lylian mythological play by a process of differentiation. It may be that our author increased the pastoral element as the arcadian fashion came into vogue, but this argument does not hold of *Gallathea*, while we are uncertain as to the date of *Love's Metamorphosis*. None of these plays are worth considering in detail, but each has its own particular point of interest. In *Gallathea* this is the introduction of girls in boys' clothes. As far as I know, Lyly is the first to use the convenient dramatic device of disguise. How effective a trick it was, is proved by the manner in which later dramatists, and in particular Shakespeare, adopted it. Its full significance cannot be appreciated by us to-day, for the whole point of it was that the actors, who appeared as girls dressed up as boys, were, as the audience knew, really boys themselves ; a fact which doubtless increased the funniness of the situation. *The Woman in the Moon* gives us a man disguised in his wife's clothes, which is a variation of the same trick. But the importance of *The Woman* lies in its poetical form. Most Elizabethan scholars have decided that this play was Lyly's first dramatic effort, on the authority of the Prologue, which bids the audience

> " Remember all is but a poet's dream,
> The first he had in Phoebus' holy bower,
> But not the last, unless the first displease."

But the maturity and strength of the drama argue a fairly considerable experience in its author, and we shall therefore be probably more correct if we place it last instead of first of Lyly's plays, interpreting the words of the Prologue as simply implying that it was Lyly's first experiment in blank verse, inspired possibly by the example of Marlowe in *Tamburlaine* and of Shakespeare in *Love's Labour's Lost*[1]. But, whatever its date, *The Woman in the Moon* must rank among the earliest examples of blank verse in our language, and, as such, its importance is very great. In *Love's Metamorphosis* there is nothing of interest equal to those points we have noticed in the other two plays of the same class. The only remarkable thing, indeed, about it is the absence of that farcical under-current which appears in all his other

[1] Bond, III. p. 234.

plays. Mr Bond suggests, with great plausibility, that such an element had originally appeared, but that, because it dealt with dangerous questions of the time, perhaps with the *Marprelate* controversy, it was expunged.

It now remains to say a few words upon *Mother Bombie*, which forms the fourth division of Lyly's dramatic writings. Though it presents many points of similarity in detail to his other plays, its general atmosphere is so different (displaying, indeed, at times distinct errors of taste) that I should be inclined to assign it to a friend or pupil of Lyly, were it not bound up with Blount's *Sixe Court Comedies*[1], and therein said to be written by "the onely Rare Poet of that time, the wittie, comical, facetiously quicke, and unparalleled John Lilly master of arts." It is clever in construction, but undeniably tedious. It shows that Lyly had learnt much from Udall, Stevenson, and Gascoigne, and perhaps its chief point of interest is that it links these writers to the later realists, Ben Jonson, and that student of London life, who is surely one of the most charming of all the Elizabethan dramatists, whimsical and delightful Thomas Dekker. *Mother Bombie* was an experiment in the drama of realism, the realism that Nash was employing so successfully in his novels. It has been labelled as our earliest pure farce of well-constructed plot and literary form, but, though it is certainly on a much higher plane than *Roister Doister*, it would only create confusion if we denied that title to Udall's play. Yet, despite its comparative unimportance, and although it is evident that Lyly is here out of his natural element, *Mother Bombie* is interesting as showing the (to our ideas) extraordinary confusion of artistic ideals which, as I have

---

[1] For title-page, Bond, III. p. 1, date 1632.

already noticed, is the remarkable thing about the Renaissance in England. Here we have a courtier, a writer of allegories, of dream-plays, the first of our mighty line of romanticists, producing a somewhat vulgar realistic play of rustic life. There is nothing anomalous in this. "Violence and variation," which someone has described as the two essentials of the ideal life, were certainly the distinguishing marks of the New Birth; and the men of that age demanded it in their literature. The drama of horror, the drama of insanity, the drama of blood, all were found on the Elizabethan stage, and all attracted large audiences. People delighted to read accounts of contemporary crime; often these choice morsels were dished up for them by some famous writer, as Kyd did in *The Murder of John Brewer*. The taste for realism is by no means a purely 19th century product. Moreover, the Elizabethans soon wearied of sameness; only a writer of the greatest versatility, such as Shakespeare, could hope for success, or at least financial success; and it was, perhaps, in order to revive his waning popularity that Lyly took to realism. But the child of fashion is always the earliest to become out of date, and we cannot think that *Mother Bombie* did much towards improving our author's reputation.

At this point of our enquiry it will be as well to say a few words upon the lyrics which Lyly sprinkled broadcast over his plays. From an aesthetic point of view these are superior to anything else he wrote. "Foreshortened in the tract of time," his novel, his plays, have become forgotten, and it is as the author of *Cupid and my Campaspe played* that he is alone known to the lover of literature. There is no need to enter into an investigation of the numerous anonymous poems which Mr Bond has claimed for him[1]; even if we knew for certain that he was their author, they are so mediocre in themselves as to be unworthy of notice, scarcely I think of recovery. But let us turn to the songs of his dramas, of which there are 32 in all. These are, of course, unequal in merit, but the best are worthy to be ranked with Shakespeare's lyrics, and our greatest dramatist was only following Lyly's example when he introduced lyrics into his plays. I have already pointed out that music was an important element in our early comedy. Udall had introduced songs into his *Roister Doister*, and we have them also in *Gammer Gurton* and *Damon and Pithias*, but never, before Lyly's day, had they taken so prominent a part in drama, for no previous dramatist had possessed a tithe of Lyly's lyrical genius. Every condition favoured our author in this introduction of songs into his plays. He had tradition at his back ; he was intensely interested in music, and probably composed the airs himself; and lastly he was master of a choir school, and would therefore use every opportunity for displaying his pupils' voices on the stage. Too much stress, however, must not be laid upon this last condition, because Lyly had already written three songs for *Campaspe* and four for *Sapho and Phao* before he became connected with St Paul's, a fact which points again to de Vere, himself a lyrist of considerable powers, as Lyly's adviser and master. Doubts, indeed, have been cast upon Lyly's authorship of these lyrics on the ground that they are omitted from the first edition of the plays. But we need, I think, have no hesitation in accepting Lyly as their creator, since the omission in question is fully accounted for by the fact that they were probably written separately from the plays, and handed round amongst the boys

[1] Bond, III. p. 433.

together with the musical score[1]. These songs are of various kinds and of widely different value. We have, for example, the purely comic poem, probably accompanied by gesture and pantomime, such as the song of Petulus from *Midas*, beginning, "O my Teeth! deare Barber ease me," with interruptions and refrains supplied by his companion and the scornful Motto. Many of these songs, indeed, are cast into dialogue form, sometimes each page singing a verse by himself, as in "O for a Bowle of fatt canary." This last is the earliest of Lyly's wine-songs, which for swing and vigour are among some of the best in our language, reminding us irresistibly of those pagan chants of the mediaeval wandering scholar which the late Mr Symonds has collected for us in his *Wine, Woman, and Song*. The drinking song, "Io Bacchus," which occurs in *Mother Bombie*, is undoubtedly, I think, modelled on one of these earlier student compositions; the reference to the practice of throwing hats into the fire is alone sufficient to suggest it. But it is as a writer of the lyric proper that Lyly is best known. No one but Herrick, perhaps, has given us more graceful love trifles woven about some classical conceit. Mr Palgrave has familiarized us with the best, *Cupid and my Campaspe played*, but there are others only less charming than this. The same theme is employed in the following:

> "O Cupid! Monarch over Kings!
> Wherefore hast thou feet and wings?
> Is it to show how swift thou art,
> When thou would'st wound a tender heart?
> Thy wings being clipped, and feet held still,
> Thy bow so many would not kill.
> It is all one in Venus' wanton school
> Who highest sits, the wise man or the fool!

[1] Bond, I. p. 36, II. p. 265.

> Fools in love's college
> Have far more knowledge
> To read a woman over,
> Than a neat prating lover.
> Nay, 'tis confessed
> That fools please women best [1]!"

Another quotation must be permitted. This time it is no embroidered conceit, but one of those lyrics of pure nature music, of which the Renaissance poets were so lavish, touched with the fire of Spring, with the light of hope, bird-notes untroubled by doubt, unconscious of pessimism, which are therefore all the more charming for us who dwell amid sunsets of intense colouring, who can see nothing but the hectic splendours of autumn. For the melancholy nightingale the poet has surprise and admiration, no sympathy:

> "What Bird so sings, yet so does wail?
> O 'tis the ravished Nightingale.
> Jug, jug, jug, jug, tereu, she cries,
> And still her woes at Midnight rise.
> Brave prick song! who is't now we hear?
> None but the lark so shrill and clear;
> Now at heaven's gates she claps her wings,
> The Morn not waking till she sings.
> Hark, hark, with what a pretty throat
> Poor Robin-red-breast tunes his note.
> Hark how the jolly cuckoos sing
> 'Cuckoo' to welcome in the spring,
> 'Cuckoo' to welcome in the spring [2]. "

This delightful song comes from the first of Lyly's dramas, and few even of Shakespeare's lyrics can equal it. Indeed, coming as it does at the dawn of the Elizabethan era, it seems like the cuckoo herself "to welcome in the spring."

---

[1] *Mother Bombie*, Act III. Sc. III. 1–14.

[2] *Campaspe*, Act V. Sc. I. 32–44. I have modernised the spelling.

SECTION III. *Lyly's dramatic Genius and Influence.*

Having thus very briefly passed in review the various plays that Lyly bequeathed to posterity[1], we must say a few words in conclusion on their main characteristics, the advance they made upon their predecessors, and their influence on later drama.

In Lyly, it is worth noticing, England has her first professional dramatist. Unlike those who had gone before him he was no amateur, he wrote for his living, and he wrote as one interested in the technical side of the theatre. They had played with drama, producing indeed interesting experiments, but accomplishing only what one would expect from men who merely took a lay interest in the theatre, and who possessed a certain knowledge, scholastic rather than technical, of the methods of the classical playwrights. He, having probably learnt at Oxford all there was to be known concerning the drama of the ancient world, came to London, and, definitely deciding to embark upon the dramatist's career, saw and studied such *moralities* and plays as were to be seen, aided and directed by the experience and knowledge of his patron : finding in the *moralities,* allegory ; in the plays of Udall and Stevenson, farce ; in *Damon and Pithias,* a romantic play upon a classical theme ; and in Gascoigne's *Supposes,* brilliant prose dialogue. That he was induced to make such a study, and that he was enabled to carry it out so thoroughly, was due partly, I think, to his peculiar financial position. As secretary of de Vere, and later as Vice-master of St Paul's School, he was independent of the actual necessity of bread-winning, which forced

---

[1] I have said nothing of the *Maydes Metamorphosis,* as most critics are agreed in assigning it to some unknown author.

even Shakespeare to pander to the garlic-eating multitude he loathed, and wrung from him the cry,

> " Alas, 'tis true I have been here and there
> And made myself a motley to the view,
> Gored mine own thoughts, sold cheap what is most dear "...

But, on the other hand, neither post was sufficiently remunerative to secure for him the comforts, still less the luxuries, of life. His income required supplementing, if only for the sake of meeting his tobacco bill, though I have a strong suspicion that the bills sent in to him served no more useful purpose than to light his pipe. But, however, adopting the theatre as his profession, he would naturally make a serious study of dramatic art, and, having no need for constantly filling the maw of present necessity, he could undertake such a study thoroughly and at his leisure. And to this cause his peculiar importance in the history of the Elizabethan stage is mainly due. Next to Jonson, the most learned of all the dramatists, yet possessing little of their poetical capacity, he set them the most conspicuous example in technique and stage-craft, in the science of play-writing, which they would probably have been far too busy to acquire for themselves. Lyly's eight dramas formed the rough-hewn but indispensable foundation-stone of the Elizabethan edifice. Spenser has been called the poet's poet, Lyly was in his own days the playwright's dramatist.

Of his dramatic construction we have already spoken. We have noticed that he introduced the art of disguise; that he varied his action by songs, accompanied perhaps with pantomime. Mr Bond suggests further that he probably did much to extend the use of stage properties and scenery[1]. But the real importance of his plays lies

---

[1] Bond, II. pp. 265–266.

in their plot construction and character drawing, points which as yet we have only touched upon. The way in which he manages the action of his plays shows a skill quite unapproached by anything that had gone before, and more pronounced than that of many which came after. Too often indeed we have dialogues, scenes, and characters which have no connexion with the development of the story; but when we consider how frequently Shakespeare sinned in this respect, we cannot blame Lyly for introducing a philosophical discussion between Plato and Aristotle, as in *Campaspe*, or those merry altercations between his pages which added so much colour and variety to his plays. However many interruptions there were, he never allowed his audience to forget the main business, as Dekker, for example, so frequently did. Nowhere, again, in Lyly's plays are the motives inadequate to support the action, as they were in the majority of dramas previous to 1580. Even Alexander's somewhat tame surrender of Campaspe is quite in accordance with his royal dignity and magnanimity; and, moreover, we are warned in the third act that the King's love is slight and will fade away at the first blast of the war trumpet, for as he tells us he is "not so far in love with Campaspe as with Bucephalus, if occasion serve either of conflict or of conquest[1]." In *Endymion* the motives are perhaps most skilfully displayed, and lead most naturally on to the action, and in this play, also, Lyly is perhaps most successful in creating that dramatic excitement which is caused by working up to an apparent deadlock (due to the intrigues of Tellus), and which is made to resolve itself and disappear in the final act. Closely allied with the development of action by the presentation of motives

[1] *Campaspe*, Act III. Sc. IV. 31.

is the weaving of the plot. And in this Lyly is not so satisfactory, though, of course, far in advance of his predecessors. A steady improvement, however, is discernible as he proceeds. In the earlier plays the page element does little more than afford comic relief: the encounters between Manes and his friends, and between Manes and his master, can hardly be dignified by the name of plot. It is in *Midas*, as I have already suggested, that this farcical under-current displays incident and action of its own, turning as it does upon the relations of the pages with Motto and the theft of the beard. Here again the comic scenes, now connected together for the first time, are also united with the main story. But the page element by no means represents Lyly's only attempt at creating an underplot. It will be seen from the story of *Endymion* related above that in that play our author is not contented with a single passion-nexus, if the expression may be allowed, that of Tellus, Cynthia, and Endymion, but he gives us another, that of Eumenides and Semele, which has no real connexion with the action, but which seriously threatens to interrupt it at one point. Other interests are hinted at, rather than developed, by the infatuation of Sir Tophas for Dipsas, and by the history of the latter's husband. Though *Midas* is more advanced in other ways, it displays nothing like the complexity of *Endymion*, and it is moreover, as I have said, cut in two by the want of connexion between the incident of the golden touch and that of the ass's ears. Lastly, in *Love's Metamorphosis*, which is without the element of farce, the relations between the nymphs and the shepherds complete that underplot of passion which is hinted at in *Sapho*, in the evident fancy which Mileta shows for Phao, and developed as we have just noticed in *Endymion*.

In this plot construction and interweaving, Lyly had no models except the classics, and we may, therefore, say that his work in this direction was almost entirely original. The last-mentioned play was produced at Court some time before 1590, and we cannot doubt, was attended by our greatest dramatist. At any rate the lessons which Shakespeare learnt from Lyly in the matter of plot complication are visible in the *Midsummer Night's Dream*, which was produced in 1595[1]. The intricate mechanism of this play, reminding us with its four plots (the Duke and Hippolyta, the lovers, the mechanics, and the fairies) of the *miracle* with its imposing but unimportant divinities in the Rood gallery, its main stage whereon moved human characters, its Crypt supplying the rude comic element in the shape of devils, and its angels who moved from one level to another welding the whole together, was far beyond Lyly's powers, but it was only possible even for Shakespeare after a thorough study of Lyly's methods.

As I have previously pointed out, Lyly was not very successful in the matter of character drawing. Never, even for a moment, is passion allowed to disturb the cultured placidity of the dialogue. The conditions under which his plays were produced may in part account for this. The children of Paul's could hardly be expected to display much light and shade of emotion in their acting, certainly depth of passion was beyond their scope. But the fault, I think, lies rather in the dramatist than in the actors. Lyly's mind was in all probability altogether of too superficial a nature for a sympathetic analysis of the human soul. That at least is how I interpret his character. All his work was more " art than nature," some of it was " more labour than art." On the

---

[1] Sidney Lee, *Life*, p. 151.

technical side his dramatic advance is immense, but we may look in vain in his dramas for any of that appreciation of the elemental facts of human nature which can alone create enduring art. In their characterization, Lyly's plays do little more than form a link between Shakespeare and the old *morality*. This comes out most strongly in their peculiar method of character grouping. By a very natural process the *moral* type is split up with the intention of giving it life and variety. Thus we have those groups of pages, of maids-in-waiting, of shepherds, of deities, etc., which are so characteristic of Lyly's plays. There is no real distinction between page and page, and between nymph and nymph ; but their merry conversations give a piquancy and colour to the drama which make up for, and in part conceal, the absence of character. All that was necessary for the creation of character was to fit these pieces of the *moral* type together again in a different way, and to breathe the spirit of genius into the new creation. We can see Lyly feeling towards this solution of the problem in his portrayal of Gunophilus, the clown of *The Woman in the Moon*. This character, which anticipates the immortal clowns of Shakespeare, is formed by an amalgamation of the pages in the previous plays into one comic figure. But Lyly also attempts to create single figures, in addition to these group characters which for the most part have little to do with the action. Often he helps out his poverty of invention by placing descriptions of one character in the mouth of another. " How stately she passeth bye, yet how soberly ! " exclaims Alexander watching Campaspe at a distance, " a sweet consent in her countenance with a chaste disdaine, desire mingled with coyness, and I cannot tell how to tearme it, a curst yeelding modestie ! "— an excellent piece of description, and one which is very necessary for the animation of the shadowy Campaspe. At times however Lyly can dispense with such adventitious aids. Pipenetta, the fascinating little wench in *Midas* and one of our dramatist's most successful creations, needs no other illumination than her own pert speeches. Diogenes again is an effective piece of work. But both these are minor characters who therefore receive no development, and if we look at the more important personages of Lyly's portrait gallery, we must agree with Mr Bond[1] that Tellus is the best. She is a character which exhibits considerable development, and she is also Lyly's only attempt to embody the evil principle in woman—a hint for the construction of that marvellous portrait of another Scottish queen, the Lady Macbeth, which Lyly just before his death in 1606 may have seen upon the stage.

On the whole Lyly is most successful when he is drawing women, which was only as it should be, if we allow that the feminine element is the very pivot of true comedy. This he saw, and it is because he was the first to realise it and to grapple with the difficulties it entailed that the title of father of English comedy may be given him without the least reserve or hesitation. Sapho the haughty but amorous queen, Mileta the mocking but tender Court lady, Gallathea the shy provincial lass, and Pipenetta the saucy little maid-servant, fill our stage for the first time in history with their tears and their laughter, their scorn of the mere male and their "curst yeelding modestie," their bold sallies and their bashful blushes. Nothing like this had as yet been seen in English literature. I have already pointed out why it was that woman asserted her place in art at this juncture. Yet, although the revolution would have come about in

[1] Bond, II. p. 284.

any case, all honour must be paid to the man who saw it coming, anticipated it, and determined its fortunes by the creation of such a number of feminine characters from every class in the social scale. And if it be true that he only gave us "their outward husk of wit and raillery and flirtation," if it be true that his interpretation of woman was superficial, that he had no understanding for the soul behind the social mask, for the emotional and passionate current, now a quiet stream, now a raging torrent, beneath the layer of etiquette, his work was none the less important for that.

> "Blood and brain and spirit, three
> Join for true felicity."

Blood his girls had and brain, but his genius was not divine enough to bestow upon them the third essential. Yet they were alive, they were flesh, they had wit, and in this they are undoubtedly the forerunners not only of Shakespeare's heroines but of Congreve's and of Meredith's—to mention the three greatest delineators of women in our language. They are the Undines in the story of our literature, beautiful and seductive, complete in everything but soul!

While realising that woman should be the real protagonist in comedy, Lyly also appreciated the fact that skilful dialogue and brilliant repartee are only less important, and that for this purpose prose was more suitable than verse. Gascoigne's *Supposes* was his model in both these innovations, and yet he would undoubtedly have adopted them of his own accord without any outside suggestion. And since *The Supposes* was a translation, *Campaspe* deserves the title of the first purely English comedy in prose. The *Euphues* had given him a reputation for sprightly and witty dialogue, he himself was possibly known at Court as a brilliant conversationalist, and therefore when he came to write plays he would naturally do all in his power to maintain and to improve his fame in this respect. With his acute sense of form he would recognise how clumsy had been the efforts of previous dramatists, and he knew also how impossible it would be, in verse form, to write witty dialogue, up to date in the subjects it handled. He therefore determined to use prose, and, though he manipulates it somewhat awkwardly in his earlier plays while still under the influence of the euphuistic fashion, he steadily improves, as he gains experience of the function and needs of dialogue, until at length he succeeds in creating a thoroughly serviceable dramatic instrument. This departure was a great event in English literature. Shakespeare was too much of a poet ever to dispense altogether with verse, but he appreciated the virtue of prose as a vehicle of comic dialogue, and he uses it occasionally even in his earliest comedy, *Love's Labour's Lost*. Ben Jonson on the other hand—perhaps more than any other Lyly's spiritual heir—wrote nearly all his comedies in prose. And it is not fanciful I think to see in Lyly's pointed dialogue, tinged with euphuism, the forerunner of Congreve's sparkling conversation and of the epigrammatic writing of our modern English playwrights.

Such are the main characteristics of Lyly's dramatic genius. To attempt to trace his influence upon later writers would be to write a history of the Elizabethan stage. In the foregoing remarks I have continually indicated Shakespeare's debt to him in matters of detail. *The Midsummer Night's Dream* is from beginning to end full of reminiscences from the plays of the earlier dramatist, transmuted, vitalized, and beautified by the genius of our greatest poet. It is as if he had witnessed in one

day a representation of all Lyly's dramatic work, and
wearied by the effort of attention had fallen asleep and
dreamt this *Dream. Love's Labour's Lost* is only less
indebted to Lyly; indeed nearly all Shakespeare's plays,
certainly all his comedies, exhibit the same influence :
for he knew his Lyly through and through, and his
assimilative power was unequalled. Shakespeare might
almost be said to be a combination of Marlowe and Lyly
plus that indefinable something which made him the
greatest writer of all time. Marlowe, his master in
tragedy, was also his master in poetry, in that strength
of conception and beauty of execution which together
make up the soul of drama. Lyly, besides the lesson he
taught him in comedy, was also his model for dramatic
construction, brilliancy of dialogue, technical skill, and all
that comprises the science of play-making—things which
were perhaps of more moment to him, with his scanty
classical knowledge, than Marlowe's lesson which he had
little need of learning. And what we have said of
Shakespeare may be said of Elizabethan drama as a
whole. "Marlowe's place," writes Mr Havelock Ellis,
"is at the heart of English poetry"; his "high, astound-
ing terms" took the world of his day by storm, his gift
to English literature was the gift of sublime beauty, of
imagination, and passion. Lyly could lay claim to none
of these, but his contribution was perhaps of more importance still. He did the spade-work, and did it once
and for all. With his knowledge of the Classics and of
previous English experiments he wrote plays that, com-
pared with what had gone before, were models of plot
construction, of the development of action, and even of
characterization. Moreover he was before Marlowe by
some nine years in the production of true romantic
drama, and in his treatment of women. In spite, there-

fore, of Marlowe's immense superiority to him on the aesthetic side, Lyly must be placed above the author of *Edward II.* in dynamical importance.

In connexion with Lyly's influence the question of the exact nature of his dramatic productions is worth a moment's consideration. Are they masques or dramas? and if the latter are they strictly speaking classical or romantic in form? As I have already suggested, the answer to the first half of this question is that they were neither and both. In Lyly's day drama had not yet been differentiated from masque, and his plays, therefore, partook of the nature of both. Produced as they were for the Court, it was natural that they should possess something of that atmosphere of pageantry, music, and pantomime which we now associate with the word masque. But Elizabeth was economical and preferred plain drama to the expensive masque displays, though she was ready to enjoy the latter, if they were provided for her by Leicester or some other favourite. Lyly's work therefore never advanced very far in the direction of the masque, though in its complimentary allegories it had much in common with it. The question as to whether it should be described as classical rather than as romantic is not one which need detain us long. It is interesting however as it again brings out the peculiarity of Lyly's position. It may indeed be claimed for him that all sections of Elizabethan drama, except perhaps tragedy, are to be found in embryo in his plays. I have said that he was the first of the romanticists, but he was no less the first important writer of classical drama. *Gorbuduc* and its like had been tedious and clumsy imitations, and, moreover, they had imitated Seneca, who was a late classic. Lyly, though the Greek dramatists were unknown to him, had probably studied Aristotle's

Poetics, and was certainly acquainted with Horace's *Ars Poetica*, and with the comedies of Terence and Plautus. He was, therefore, an authority on matters dramatic, and could boast of a learning on the subject of technique which few of his contemporaries or his successors could lay claim to, and which they were only too ready to glean second-hand. And yet, though he was wise enough to appreciate all that the classics could teach him, he was a romanticist at heart, or perhaps it would be better to say that he threw the beautiful and loosely fitting garment of romanticism over the classical frame of his dramas. And even in the matter of this frame he was not always orthodox. He bowed to the tradition of the unities: but he frequently broke with it; in *The Woman* alone does he confine the action to one day; and, though he is more careful to observe unity of place, imaginary transfers occurring in the middle of scenes indicate his rebellion against this restriction. Nevertheless, when all is said, he remains, with the exception of Jonson, the most classical of all Elizabethan playwrights, and just as he anticipates the 17th and 18th centuries in his prose, so in his dramas we may discover the first competent handling of those principles and restrictions which, more clearly enunciated by Ben Jonson, became iron laws for the post-Elizabethan dramatists.

It is this "balance between classic precedent and romantic freedom[1]" that constitutes his supreme importance, not only in Elizabethan literature, but even in the history of subsequent English drama. From Lyly we may trace the current of romanticism, through Shakespeare, to Goethe and Victor Hugo; in Lyly also we may see the first embodiment of that classical tradition which even Shakespeare's "purge" could do

[1] Bond, II. p. 266.

nothing to check, and which was eventually to lay its dead hand upon the art of the 18th century. May we not say more than this? Is he not the first name in a continuous series from 1580 to our own day, the first link in the chain of dramatic development, which binds the "singing room of Powles" to the Lyceum of Irving? And it is interesting to notice that the principle which he was the first to express shows at the present moment evident signs of exhaustion; for its future developments seem to be limited to that narrow strip of social melodrama, which lies between the devil of the comic opera and the deep sea of the Ibsenic problem play. Indeed it would not be altogether fanciful, I think, to say that *The Importance of being Earnest* finishes the process that *Campaspe* started; and to view that process as a circle begun in euphuism, and completed in aestheticism.

CHAPTER IV.

CONCLUSION.

AT the beginning of this essay I gave a short account of the main facts of our author's life, reserving my judgment upon his character and genius until after the examination of his works. That examination which I have now concluded is far too superficial in character to justify a psychological synthesis such as that advocated by M. Hennequin[1]. But though this essay cannot claim to have exhausted the subject of the ways and means of Lyly's art, yet in the course of our survey we have had occasion to notice several interesting points in reference to his mind and character, which it will be well to bring together now in order to give a portrait, however inadequate, of the man who played so important a part in English literature.

Nash supplies the only piece of contemporary information about his person and habits, and all he tells us is that he was short of stature and that he smoked. But Ben Jonson gives us an unmistakeable caricature of him under the delightfully appropriate name of Fastidious Brisk in *Every Man out of His Humour*. He describes him as a " neat, spruce, affecting courtier, one that wears clothes well, and in fashion ; practiseth

[1] *La Critique Scientifique.*

by his glass how to salute ; speaks good remnants not-
withstanding his base viol and tobacco ; swears tersely
and with variety ; cares not what lady's favour he belies,
or great man's familiarity : a good property to perfume
the boot of a coach. He will borrow another man's
horse to praise and back him as his own. Or, for a need
can post himself into credit with his merchant, only with
the gingle of his spur and the jerk of his wand[1]."
Allowing for the exaggeration of satire, we cannot
doubt that this portrait is in the main correct.   It
indicates a man who follows fashion, even in swearing,
to the excess of foppery, who delights in scandal, who
contracts debts with an easy conscience, and who is
withal a merry fellow and a wit.   All this is in accordance with what we know of his life. We can picture
him at Oxford serenading the Magdalen dons with his
" base viol," or perhaps organizing a night party to
disturb the slumbers of some insolent tradesman who
had dared to insist upon payment ; his neat little figure
leading a gang of young rascals, and among them the
" sea-dog " Hakluyt, the sturdy and as yet unconverted
Gosson, the refined Watson, and perchance George
Pettie concealing his thorough enjoyment of the situation by a smile of elderly amusement.   Or yet again we
can see him at the room of some boon companion
seriously announcing to a convulsed assembly his intention of applying for a fellowship, and when the last
quip had been hurled at him through clouds of smoke
and the laughter had died down, proposing that the
house should go into committee for the purpose of
concocting the now famous letter to Burleigh. When
we next catch a glimpse of him he is no longer the
madcap ; he walks with such dignity as his stature

[1] From the *Preface*.

permits, for he is now author of the much-talked-of *Anatomy of Wit*, and one of the most fashionable young men of the Court. What elaboration of toilet, what adjustment and readjustment of ruffles and lace, what bowing and scraping before the glass, preceded that great event of his life—his presentation to the Queen—can only be guessed at. But we can well picture him, following his magnificently over-dressed patron up the long reception-room, his heart beating with pleasurable excitement, yet his manners not forgotten in the hour of his pride, as he nods to an acquaintance and bows with sly demureness to some Iffida or Camilla. Those were the days of his success, the happiest period of his life when, as secretary to the Lord Chamberlain and associate of the highest in the land, he breathed his native atmosphere, the praises and flattery of a fickle world of fashion. But, time-server as he was, he was no sycophant. Leaving de Vere's service after a sharp quarrel, he was not ashamed to take up the profession of teaching in which he had already had some experience. We see him next, therefore, a master of St Paul's, engrossed in the not unpleasant duties of drilling his pupils for the performance of his plays, accompanying their songs on his instrument, or himself taking his place on the stage, now as Diogenes in his ubiquitous tub, and now as the golden-bearded and long-eared Midas. And last of all he appears as the disappointed, disillusioned man, "infelix academicus ignotus." A wife and children on his hands, his occupation gone, his hopes of the Revels Mastership blasted, he becomes desperate, and writes that last bitter letter to Elizabeth.

The man of fashion out of date, the social success left high and dry by the unheeding current, he died eventually in poverty, not because he had wasted his

substance, like Greene, in Bohemia, but because, thinking
to take Belgravia by storm, he had forgotten that the
foundations of that city are laid on the bodies of her
sons. But leaving

> "The thrice three muses mourning for the death
> Of Learning late deceased in beggary,"

let us look more closely into the character of this man,
whose brilliant and successful youth was followed by so
sad an old age.

In spite of Professor Raleigh and the moralizing of
Euphues, we may decide that there was nothing of the
Puritan about him. His life at Oxford, his attachment
to the notorious de Vere, the keen pleasure he took in
the things of this world, are, I think, sufficient to prove
this. His general attitude towards life was one of vigorous
hedonism, not of intellectual asceticism. The ethical
element of *Euphues* links him rather to the already
vanishing Humanism than to the rising Puritanism,
against which all his sympathies were enlisted, as his
contributions to the *Marprelate* controversy indicate. I
have refrained from touching upon these *Mar-Martin*
tracts because they possess neither aesthetic nor dynamical importance, being, as Gabriel Harvey—always
ready with the spiteful epigram—describes them, "ale-
house and tinkerly stuffe, nothing worthy a scholar or a
real gentleman." They are worth mentioning, however,
as throwing a light upon the religious prejudices of our
author. He was a courtier and he was a churchman, and
in lending his aid to crush sectarians he thought no more
deeply about the matter than he did in voting as Member
of Parliament against measures which conflicted with his
social inclinations. There was probably not an ounce of
the theological spirit in his whole composition ; for his
refutation of atheism was a youthful essay in dialectics,

a bone thrown to the traditions of the moral Court treatise.

If, indeed, he was seriously minded in any respect, it was upon the subject of Art. Himself a novelist and dramatist, he displayed also a keen delight in music, and evinced a considerable, if somewhat superficial, interest in painting. And yet, though he apparently made it his business to know something of every art, he was no sciolist, and, if he went far afield, it was only in order to improve himself in his own particular branch. All the knowledge he acquired in such amateur appreciation was brought to the service of his literary productions. And the same may be said of his extensive excursions into the land of books. No Elizabethan dramatist but Lyly, with the possible exception of Jonson, could marshal such an array of learning, and few could have turned even what they had with such skill and effect to their own purposes. Lyly had made a thorough study of such classics as were available in his day, and we have seen how he employed them in his novel and in his plays. But the classics formed only a small section of the books digested by this omnivorous reader. If he could not read Spanish, French, or Italian, he devoured and assimilated the numerous translations from those languages into English, Guevara indeed being his chief inspiration. Nor did he neglect the literature of his own land. Few books we may suppose, which had been published in English previous to 1580, had been unnoticed by him. We have seen what a thorough acquaintance he possessed of English drama before his day, and how he exhibits the influence of the writings of Ascham and perhaps other humanists, how he laid himself under obligation to the bestiaries and the proverb-books for his euphuistic philosophy, and how his lyrics indicate a possible study of the mediaeval scholar song-books. In conclusion, it is interesting to notice that we have clear evidence that he knew Chaucer[1].

Idleness, therefore, cannot be urged against him; nor does this imposing display of learning indicate a pedant. Lyly had nothing in common with the spirit of his old friend Gabriel Harvey, whom indeed he laughed at. There is a story that Watson and Nash invited a company together to sup at the Nag's Head in Cheapside, and to discuss the pedantries of Harvey, and our euphuist in all probability made one of the party. His erudition sat lightly on him, for it was simply a means to the end of his art. Moreover, a student's life could have possessed no attraction for one of his temperament. Unlike Marlowe and Greene, he had harvested all his wild oats before he left Oxford; but the process had refined rather than sobered him, for his laugh lost none of its merriment, and his wit improved with experience, so that we may well believe that in the Court he was more Philautus than Euphues. In his writings also his aim was to be graceful rather than erudite; and, ponderous as his *Euphues* seems to us now, it appealed to its Elizabethan public as a model of elegance. His art was perhaps only an instrument for the acquisition of social success, but he was nevertheless an artist to the fingertips. Yet he was without the artist's ideals, and this fact, together with his frivolity, vitiated his writings to a considerable extent, or, rather, the superficiality of his art was the result of the superficiality of his soul. Of that "high seriousness," which Aristotle has declared to be the poet's essential, he has nothing. Technique throughout was his chief interest, and it is in technique alone that he can claim to have succeeded. "More art than

[1] Bond, I. p. 401.

nature " is a just criticism of everything he wrote, with
the exception of his lyrics.   He was supremely clever,
one of the cleverest writers in our literature when we
consider what he accomplished, and how small was the
legacy of his predecessors ; but he was much too clever
to be simple.   He excelled in the niceties of art, he
revelled in the accomplishment of literary feats, his
intellect was akin to the intellect of those who in their
humbler fashion find pleasure in the solution of acrostics.
And consequently his writings were frequently as finical
as his dress was fastidious ; for it was the form and not
the idea which fascinated him ; to his type of mind the
letter was everything and the spirit nothing.   Indeed,
the true spirit of art was quite beyond his comprehension,
though he was connoisseur enough to appreciate its presence in others.   Artist and man of taste he was, but he
was no poet.   Artist he was, I have said, to the fingertips, but his art lay at his fingers' ends, not at his soul.
He was facile, ingenious, dexterous, everything but inspired.   He had wit, learning, skill, imagination, but
none of that passionate apprehension of life which
makes the poet, and which Marlowe and Shakespeare
possessed so fully.   And therefore it was his fate to be
nothing more than a forerunner, a straightener of the
way ; and before his death he realised with bitterness
that he was only a stepping-stone for young Shakespeare
to mount his throne.   He was, indeed, the draughtsman
of the Elizabethan workshop, planning and designing
what others might build.   He was the expert mathematician who formulated the laws which enabled Shakespeare
to read the stars.   Of the heights and depths of passion
he was unconscious ; he was no psychologist, laying bare
the human soul with the lancet ; and though now and
again, as in *Endymion*, he caught a glimpse of the silver

beauties of the moon, he had no conception of the glories of the midday sun.

And yet though he lacked the poet's sense, his wit did something to repair the defect, and even if it has a musty flavour for our pampered palates, it saves his writings from becoming unbearably wearisome ; and moreover his fun was without that element of coarseness which mars the comic scenes of later dramatists who appealed to more popular audiences. But it is quite impossible for us to realise how brilliant his wit seemed to the Elizabethans before it was eclipsed by the genius of Shakespeare. Even as late as 1632 Blount exclaims, "This poet sat at the sunne's table," words referring perhaps more especially to Lyly's poetical faculty, but much truer if interpreted as an allusion to his wit. The genius of our hero played like a dancing sunbeam over the early Elizabethan stage. Never before had England seen anything like it, and we cannot wonder that his public hailed him in their delight as one of the greatest writers of all time. How could they know that he was only the first voice in a choir of singers which, bursting forth before his notes had died away, would shake the very arch of heaven with the passion and the beauty of their song? But for us who have heard the chorus first, the recitative seems poor and thin. The magic has long passed from *Euphues*, once a name to conjure with, and even the plays seem dull and lifeless. That it should be so was inevitable, for the wit which illuminated these works was of the time, temporary, the earliest beam of the rising sun. This sunbeam it is impossible to recover, and with all our efforts we catch little but dust.

And yet for the scientific critic Lyly's work is still alive with significance. Worthless as much of it is from the aesthetic point of view, from the dynamical, the historical aspect few English writers are of greater interest. Waller was rescued from oblivion and labelled as the first of the classical poets. But we can claim more for Lyly than this. Extravagant as it may sound, he was one of the great founders of our literature. His experiments in prose first taught men that style was a matter worthy of careful study, he was among the earliest of those who realised the utility of blank verse for dramatic purposes, he wrote the first English novel in our language, and finally he is not only deservedly recognised as the father of English comedy, but by his mastery of dramatic technique he laid such a burden of obligation upon future playwrights that he placed English drama upon a completely new basis. Of the three main branches of our literature, therefore, two—the novel and the drama—were practically of his creation, and though his work suffered because it lacked the quality of poetry, for the historian of literature it is none the less important on that account.

LIST OF CHIEF AUTHORITIES.

ARBER. The Martin Marprelate Controversy. Scholar's Library.

ASCHAM, ROGER. The Schoolmaster. Arber's English Reprints.

„ „ Toxophilus. „ „ „

BAKER, G. P. Lyly's Endymion.

BARNEFIELD, RICHARD. Poems. Arber's Scholar's Library.

BERNERS, LORD. The Golden Boke of Marcus Aurelius.

„ „ Froissart's Chronicles. Globe Edition.

BOAS. Works of Kyd. Clarendon Press.

BOND, R. W. John Lyly. „ „ 3 Vols.

BRUNET. Manuel de Libraire.

BUTLER CLARKE. Spanish Literature.

CHILD, C. G. John Lyly and Euphuism. *Münchener Beiträge* VII.

CRAIK, SIR H. Specimens of English Prose.

DICTIONARY of National Biography.

EARLE. History of English Prose.

FIELD, NATHANIEL. A Woman is a Weathercock.

FITZMAURICE-KELLY. Spanish Literature. Heinemann.

GAYLEY. Representative English Comedies.

GOSSE. From Shakespeare to Pope.

GOSSON. School of Abuse. Arber's English Reprints.

GUEVARA, ANTONIO DE. Libro Aureo del emperado Marco Aurelio.

HALLAM. Introduction to the Literature of Europe.

HENNEQUIN. La Critique Scientifique.

HUME, MARTIN. Spanish Influence on English Literature.

JUSSERAND. The English Novel in the time of Shakespeare.

LANDMANN, DR. Shakespeare and Euphuism. *New Shak. Soc. Trans.* 1880–2.

„ „ Introduction to Euphues. Sprache und Literatur.

LATIMER. Sermons. Arber's English Reprints.

LEE, SIDNEY. Athenæum, July 14, 1883.
    „   Huon of Bordeaux (Berners'). Early Eng. Text
                Soc. Extra Series XL., XLI.
    „   Life of Shakespeare.
LIEBIG. Lord Bacon et les sciences d'observation en moyen âge.
LYLY. Euphues. Arber's English Reprints.
MACAULAY, G. G. Introd. to Froissart's Chronicles. Globe
    Edition.
MEREDITH, GEORGE. Essay on Comedy.
MÉZIÈRES. Prédécesseurs et contemporains de Shakespeare.
MINTO. Manual of English Prose Literature.
NORTH, THOMAS. Diall of Princes.
PEARSON, KARL. Chances of Death. Vol. II. *German Passion
    Play.*
PETTIE, GEORGE. Petite Palace of Pettie his Pleasure.
RALEIGH, PROF. W. The English Novel.
RETURN FROM PARNASSUS. Arber's Scholar's Library.
SAINTSBURY. Specimens of English Prose.
SPENCER, HERBERT. Essays—Philosophy of Style.
SYMONDS, J. A. Shakespeare's Predecessors.
UDALL, NICHOLAS. Ralph Roister Doister. Arber's English
    Reprints.
UNDERHILL. Spanish Literature in Tudor England.
WARD, DR A. W. English Dramatic Literature. 3 Vols.
    „   MRS H. "John Lyly," Article in *Enc. Brit.*
WATSON, THOMAS. Poems. Arber's English Reprints.
WEBBE. Discourses of English Poetry. Arber's English Re-
    prints.
WEYMOUTH, DR R. F. On Euphuism. *Phil. Soc. Trans.*
    1870–2.

INDEX.